Also by Chris Jennings

HIV/AIDS

The Facts and The Fiction

Understanding and Preventing AIDS:
A Book for Everyone

(*Or, everything you always wanted to know about HIV/AIDS, but were afraid to ask*)

HIV/AIDS in South Africa:

The Facts

and

The Fiction

Health Alert
Communications HAC

Disclaimer

Any statement made in this document is not unequivocal. Data may exist in other databases which countermand the data presented here. All data are subject to change as scientific and medical knowledge and technology advance. Any interpretation of this data set and/or the actions purportedly undertaken by any individuals and/or organizations are open to question and/or alternate interpretation.

ISBN-10: 0-936571-08-X
ISBN-13: 978-0-936571-08-9
Version 1.1 (2019)

HAC

Health Alert Communications
Cambridge, Massachusetts
(617) 497-4190
www.healthalert.net

Table of Contents

List of Tables

List of Figures

Abbreviations and Definitions

AIDS	Acquired immunodeficiency syndrome
AIDS prodrome	Vague malaise prior to m of opportunistic infections
Algorithm	Step-by-step procedure for diagnosing medical conditions
Antigen	Substance or object that triggers the creation of antibodies
Assay	Test for determining the amount of a particular constituent
Asymptomatic	Without symptoms
Candida albicans	Fungus common to human mucous membranes
Candidiasis	Disease caused by the fungus *Candida albicans*
CD4	T4-lymphocyte (a.k.a. T4-cell or helper cell)
CD4/CD8 ratio	Ratio of CD4 to CD8 lymphocytes
CD8	T8-lymphocyte (a.k.a. T8-cell or suppresser cell)
CDC	Centers for Disease Control (and Prevention)
Cell-mediated immunity	Immune response involving T lymphocytes
Cellular immunity	Immune response involving T lymphocytes
Clinical	As seen in the doctor's office, i.e., not laboratory findings
CNS	Central nervous system (the brain and spinal cord)
Cohort	A group of individuals who share a characteristic
Cryptosporidiosis	Enteric disease caused by the protozoan Cryptosporidium
DOH	Department of Health (in the Republic of South Africa)
Endemic	Native to particular people, locality, region, or country
Enteric	Relating to the intestine
Epidemiology	Study of disease in populations
Etiology	Cause of a disease or abnormal condition
Hematological	Relating to the blood
HIV	Human immunodeficiency virus
HIV disease	Morbidity consequent to HIV infection as defined by ICD-10
Humeral immunity	Immune response involving antibodies
ICD-10	International Classification of Diseases (10th edition)
Incubation	Time of infection before opportunistic disease onset
KS	Kaposi's sarcoma
KSHV	Kaposi's sarcoma herpes virus
Lymphadenopathy	Abnormal enlargement of the lymph nodes (glands)
Mycobacterium tuberculosis	Bacterium responsible for tuberculosis
Pathogenic	Disease-causing
PCP	*Pneumocystis carinii* pneumonia
Platelets	Components of the blood that assist blood clotting
PLWH	People living with HIV

Pneumocystis carinii	Yeast-like fungus causing *Pneumocystis carinii* pneumonia
Primates	Monkeys, apes (and humans)
Prophylaxis	Preventative therapy
Protozoan	Multiple-cellular organism
Retrovirus	RNA-based virus that replicates via a DNA intermediate
RSA	Republic of South Africa
Serological	Relating to serum
Seroconversion	Conversion from negative to positive in HIV blood test
Seropositive	Positive serum reaction for presence of antibody
Serum	Fluid part of the blood
Statistics South Africa	RSA agency responsible for statistical collection and reporting
T-cell	T lymphocyte
T4-cell	T helper cells – primary site of HIV infection (a.k.a. CD4)
T4/T8 ratio	Ratio of T4 to T8 lymphocytes (a.k.a. CD4/CD8)
T8-cell	T suppressor cell; counters action of the T4-cell (a.k.a. CD8)
Thrombocytopenia	Lack of platelets; possibly an AIDS-related condition
Toxoplasma gondii	Protozoal parasite, commonly infects CNS of AIDS patients
Toxoplasmosis	Disease caused by a protozoal parasite *Toxoplasma gondii*
UNAIDS	Joint United Nations Programme on HIV/AIDS
WHO	World Health Organization

Preface

In preparation for this book, **HIV/AIDS in South Africa – The Facts and The Fiction**, and the primary work to which this work is adjuvant, **HIV/AIDS – The Facts and The Fiction**, the Author reviewed more than 3,000 scientific and medical articles.

The scientific literature is not all-encompassing. Nor is it particularly methodical in its acquisition of knowledge. It is a collection of works by various authors having a myriad of differing approaches, disciplines, and agendas. Nevertheless, the scientific and medical literatures represent, at best, the collective embodiment of scientific and medical knowledge, as well as the framework and justification for medical and/or societal interventions.

Given a sober review, the scientific literature is clear: (1) New York City is the epicenter of the AIDS epidemic; (2) the theory that HIV came from monkeys is a fallacy; and (3) the African AIDS epidemic-as-holocaust never manifested.

Unfortunately, a series of interlocking fallacies have distorted scientific and public perceptions of HIV and the AIDS epidemic. In this distortion, the basic theorem for the origin-of-AIDS-in-Africa hypothesis is that HIV was endemic in Africa for 30 or 40 years before ecological and sociological changes forced it out of the jungle. Once exposed to naïve, urban, highly susceptible populations, the disease spread exponentially; eventually infecting tens or hundreds of millions of Africans (without anybody noticing) before reaching across the Atlantic to selectively infect gay men in New York City. This theory forms the foundation of scientific belief and, as such, has created a belief structure such that scientific and medical data are viewed as through a warped lens.

The goal of this work is to reconfigure the conceptual paradigm of the HIV/AIDS epidemic, such that resource allocations and health care interventions work to serve the benefit, and not the detriment, of the populations at need. As such, the work attempts to address all the relevant disciplines, present information previously overlooked, and reconfigure the AIDS scenario into a new conceptual constellation, the constellation depicted by the medical and scientific literature.

This book should not be considered the definitive work on HIV/AIDS — a project beyond the capability of any one person. Ideally, this book is a starting point for new investigations. Although the book contains many numbers, it should be viewed as a qualitative work and not a quantitative work. Its contents are derived principally from the scientific literature, but the scientific literature is not a perfect lens for viewing the world; nor is the Author a perfect medium for communicating the vastness of this collective knowledge.

For people unfamiliar with the concept, the method of grading in school systems can be quantitative or qualitative. A *quantitative* grading system assigns numerical grades to student scores. A *qualitative* grading system scores the outcome only as *Pass* or *Fail* (alternately as *Good, Fair,* or *Poor*, etc.). Therefore, after reading this book, one should be able to determine whether the current conceptual paradigm of the HIV/AIDS epidemic receives a passing or failing grade.

Sometimes the Author is viewed as seemingly uncaring in his discourse. The Author would like to apologize in advance should he hurt the feelings of anyone who has suffered a personal loss to AIDS. From the remote position as researcher and writer, the Author fears that he writes dispassionately, but hopefully, too, also from a position best to describe and characterize this massive event in human history, and in a fashion that might alter our perspective and interaction with it.

The use of certain words in this document requires some explanation. The following words are used to humanize the story and simplify its rendition. These words are not meant in any way to disparage:

<u>Gay Men</u> – Generally, the gay men described in this document were the subset who were exposed to HIV and/or developed AIDS early in the epidemic. The majority of these gay men were highly sexually active. Therefore, the terms "gay men" or "homosexual males" in this document most frequently describes a subset of highly sexually active, gay men in specific geographic locales. This is not the behavior of all gay men. Not all gay men engage in high-risk sexual behavior. The term "gay men" is more colloquial than "homosexual men" or "men who have sex with men" and easier to use while writing. However, these terms are used by the Centers for Disease Control and Prevention (CDC) and most other public and private authorities discoursing on the topics and themes relating to HIV/AIDS (there being the legitimate concern that many men who have sex with both men and women do not self-identify themselves as gay).

Racial Terms – the terms used to describe race herein are the demographic terms used in the Republic of South Africa (formerly the Union of South Africa) and their demographic reports. *White* designates Caucasian; *African Black* refers to the indigenous peoples of the region, *Colored* generally to people of mixed race, but may include some Indians and Asians; and the *Indian/Asian* category is self-explanatory.

1. Introduction

Few people realize that the familiar HIV/AIDS statistics are *estimates*, not actual surveillance data: not the actual number of reported cases. Surveillance is the process by which national health authorities systematically collect data on diseases; performed by each country per internal standards, protocols, surveillance definition(s) of disease(s), and capabilities.

The estimates are derived from mathematical models. These estimates are the numbers inserted into maps and slide shows, widely distributed by the World Health Organization (**WHO**) and the Joint United Nations Programme on HIV/AIDS (**UNAIDS**). Echoed further by the public and scientific media, these figures prevail in public and professional perceptions.

This book provides a service by presenting and comparing actual surveillance data with these familiar WHO/UNAIDS estimates. Surveillance data are rarely widely distributed; thus, the discrepancies between the estimates and other sources of surveillance data are rarely noted. The Republic of South Africa (RSA) stands as the principal exemplar of this discrepancy, as seen in Table 1.

Table 1 - RSA death notifications compared with UNAIDS estimates

Year	UNAIDS Estimate People living with HIV/AIDS Republic of South Africa	UNAIDS Estimate AIDS Deaths Republic of South Africa	AIDS Deaths per RSA Death Notifications
1997	2 900 000 [1]	140 000 [1]	6 235 [2]
1999	4 200 000 [3]	250 000 [3]	9 935 [2]
2001	4 700 000 [4]	180 000 [4]	9 244 [2]
	4 600 000 [5]	220 000 [5]	9 244 [2]
	5 000 000 [6]	360 000 [6]	9 244 [2]
2007	5 700 000 [4]	350 000 [4]	13 521 [7]
2008	5 300 000 [8]	— [8]	15 097 [9]
2009	5 600 000 [5]	310 000 [5]	*n.a.*

UNAIDS estimates include Adults & Children

Given the most recent UNAIDS estimate (2009), the Republic of South Africa (RSA) had an estimated 5.6 million people living with HIV/AIDS — "the largest [HIV/AIDS epidemic] in the world."[5, 10]

The current situation is best clarified by an examination of the past. In 1997, per UNAIDS estimate, the RSA had 2.9 million *people living with HIV* (**PLWH**).[1] Allowing for the mean 11-year survival period imputed into the mathematical models that generate these estimates, a substantial cluster of these people should have died by 2008. Yet, the RSA tabulated a total of only 136,000 HIV/AIDS deaths for years 1997 through 2008, inclusive.[2, 7, 9, 11-13]

The corresponding UNAIDS estimates for the number of HIV/AIDS deaths in the Republic of South Africa are also rather nonsensical. For example, UNAIDS estimated 140,000 HIV/AIDS deaths in the RSA for 1997.[1] Yet RSA tabulated only 6,235 HIV/AIDS deaths in 1997, followed by 7,269 HIV/AIDS deaths in 1998.[2]

Furthermore, UNAIDS estimated 250,000 HIV/AIDS in 1999 (with 4.2 million PLWH).[3] Yet the Statistics South Africa tabulated only 9,935 and 10,459 HIV/AIDS deaths in 1999 and 2000, respectively.[2] (**Statistics South Africa** is the government agency responsible for the collection, production and dissemination of official statistics, including mortality statistics. These mortality statistics are developed for the purpose of policy formation.[11])

All of the aforementioned numbers will be further qualified. In doing so, this book presents:

- raw numerical data for the number of HIV/AIDS deaths in the Republic of South Africa (RSA) as determined by Statistics South Africa in their annual tabulation of death notifications

- estimates for the HIV/AIDS deaths and the number of people living with HIV/AIDS in the RSA as generated by WHO/UNAIDS mathematical models

- raw numerical data from surveillance reports of the RSA, the United States, and from all of Africa.

Although this book clarifies the discrepancies between surveillance data and modeled estimates by describing two common misunderstandings of HIV infection that contribute to poor modeling outcomes, this book is *not* a critique of these mathematical models. Rather, this book provides a valuable service by presenting the actual surveillance data, comparing the data with the WHO/UNAIDS estimates, and placing this vast information in an appropriate context relative to the medical literature documenting the HIV/AIDS epidemic.

2. REPUBLIC OF SOUTH AFRICA (RSA) DEATH NOTIFICATIONS

In this document, all "HIV/AIDS deaths" attributed to the tabulation of RSA death notifications are defined as deaths in which HIV/AIDS has been attributed as the **underlying cause of death**.

However, the term *underlying cause of death* does not appear on the RSA death notification form. Rather, the form lists **causes of death**. The standard death notification form allows up to 5 *causes of death* to be listed. Approximately 50% of the forms list only 1 cause of death.[9] For each death notification form, the information provided by the listed *causes of death* is used to derive the *underlying cause of death*. The *underlying cause of death* is considered the final result.

This derivation is performed automatically by a software program called Automated Classification of Medical Entities (ACME 2004.02) developed by the United States National Center for Health Statistics (NCHS). This software program utilizes the International Classification of Diseases, Version 10 (ICD-10) for classifying diseases.[9, 11]

Statistics South Africa modified the ICD codes to reflect the local disease patterns, a common procedure worldwide. Health authorities tend to modify the ICD codes to best accommodate and differentiate between medical conditions common to the population(s) under observation. (Appendix A compares RSA and NCHS ranking methods top ten leading underlying causes of death in 1999.)

Statistics South Africa is the government agency responsible for the collection, production and dissemination of official statistics, including mortality statistics. These mortality statistics are developed for the purpose of policy formation.[11] Per Statistics South Africa, the exact definitions of *causes of death* and *underlying causes of death* are:

- **causes of death** are all those diseases, morbid conditions, or injuries that either resulted in or contributed to death."[9]

- **underlying cause of death** is the disease or injury that initiated the sequence of events leading directly to death, or the circumstances of the accident or violence which produced the fatal injury."[9]

Table 2 compares the *underlying cause of death* with the *causes of death*, where available. The numbers for *causes of death* represent the actual number of death notification forms that listed "**HIV disease**" as the cause of death (ICD-10 code B20-B24). Overall, the number of forms containing HIV as the *cause of death* and the number of deaths attributing HIV disease as the *underlying cause of death* are comparable.

Table 2 also lists the total annual number of all deaths due to all causes in the RSA, the percentage of HIV/AIDS deaths relative to all deaths that year, and the rank of HIV/AIDS deaths among each year's ten leading natural causes of death. Deaths from HIV/AIDS were not consistently among the top leading natural causes of death until 2005.

Table 2 – HIV/AIDS as Underlying Cause vs. Cause of Death, 1997–2008

Year	HIV Disease Determined as Underlying Cause	% of all Deaths	All Deaths*	Death Notifications reporting HIV as Cause of Death	Top Ten Rank	Ref
1997	6 235	2.0 %	317 132	—	—	2
1998	7 269	2.0 %	365 853	—	—	2
1999	9 935	2.6 %	381 820	10 331	9	2
2000	10 459	2.5 %	416 155	—	—	2
2001	9 244	2.0 %	454 882	—	—	2
2002	10 491	2.1 %	502 050	—	—	2
2003	11 650	2.1 %	556 779	11 926	—	2
2004	13 319	2.3 %	576 709	13 590	10	2
2005	14 532	2.46 %	598 131	14 865	10	12
2006	14 783	2.4 %	612 778	14 969	9	13
2007	13 521	2.2 %	603 094	13 725	9	7
2008	15 097	2.5 %	—	15 296	7	9

* Source: Mortality and causes of death in South Africa, 2008: Findings from death notification. In: Africa SS, ed. Pretoria, South Africa: Statistics South Africa, Pretoria; 2010.

(By way of sample, Appendix B compares the number of *underlying causes of death* with the number of death notification forms listing that *cause of death* for the top ten leading underlying causes of death for 1997, 1999, and 2001.)

There are many issues surrounding the collection of mortality data in the Republic of South Africa. Please be sure to read the information in Appendix C to learn more about the character and limitations of this data set. Also see Appendix D, HIV/AIDS in the RSA Health System.

3. COMPARE THE NUMBERS

3.1. AIDS Cases in the RSA compared with United States

This section presents the actual surveillance data of reported AIDS cases rather than estimates. Table 3 compares the number of reported AIDS cases in the Republic of South Africa (RSA) with the number of reported AIDS cases in the United States for the years 1981–2002. Each nation performs surveys using its own protocols. (See Appendix C for more information on the RSA data set.)

HIV infection is a notifiable disease in the United States, meaning physicians are mandated to report each incidence (but not the name of the patient) to the appropriate health authority.[14] In the RSA, HIV infection is not a notifiable disease.[15, 16]

As seen in Table 3 the RSA stopped reporting surveillance data in October 1996. At last report, RSA had 12,825 reported AIDS cases.[17] (In comparison, at the end of October 1996, the United States had close to 565,000 reported AIDS cases.)[18, 19]

In June 1998, less than 2 years after the RSA had 12,825 reported AIDS cases, WHO estimated that the RSA had 140,000 HIV/AIDS deaths during 1997, and a total of 2,900,000 people living with HIV/AIDS in 1997.[1, 17, 20]

Table 3 – AIDS cases in the RSA compared with United States

United States	Surveillance Report Date	Ref	Republic of South Africa	Surveillance Report Date	Ref
5	Jun 1981	21			
593	Sep 1982	22	2	Dec 1982	23, 24
1 641	Jun 1983	25			
4 918	Jun 1984	26			
10 000	Apr 1985	27	21	Jul 1985	28
29 003	Dec 1986	29	30	Sep 1986	28
40 845	Aug 1987	30	77	Jul 1987	30
43 533	Oct 1987	31	81	Sep 1987	31
55 167	Mar 1988	32	98	Jan 1988	32
65 099	Jun 1988	33	120	Apr 1988	33
78 985	Nov 1988	34	143	Oct 1988	34
80 538	Dec 1988	35	150	Oct 1988	35
84 503	Jan 1989	36	150	Oct 1988	36
86 656	Feb 1989	37	195	Jan 1989	37
92 719	May 1989	38	226	Apr 1989	38
95 561	May 1989	39	231	Jun 1989	39
98 255	Jun 1989	40	231	Jun 1989	40
100 885	Aug 1989	41	231	Jun 1989	41
104 210	Aug 1989	42	244	Jul 1989	42
107 308	Oct 1989	43	244	Jul 1989	43
113 211	Dec 1989	44	310	Oct 1989	44
117 781	Dec 1989	45	332	Dec 1989	45
126 127	Apr 1990	46	535	Feb 1990	46
137 385	Jul 1990	47	463	Jun 1990	47
140 822	Jul 1990	48	463	Jun 1990	48
144 221	Aug 1990	49	463	Jun 1990	49
149 498	Sep 1990	50	353	Sep 1990	50
171 876	Mar 1991	51	650	Dec 1990	51
202 843	Nov 1991	52	1 019	Nov 1991	52
242 146	Dec 1992	53	1 316	Jun 1992	53
289 320	Mar 1993	54	1 803	Feb 1993	54
339 250	Sep 1993	55	1 803	Feb 1993	55
411 907	Dec 1993	56	3 210	Feb 1994	56
401 789	Sep 1994	57	3 849	Jul 1994	57
441 528	Dec 1994	58	3 849	Jul 1994	58
501 310	Oct 1995	59	8 405	Mar 1995	59
513 486	Dec 1995	60	10 351	Aug 1995	60
565 097	Sep 1996	61	10 351	Apr 1996	61
581 429	*Dec 1996*	*17*	*12 825*	*Oct 1996*	*17*
612 078	Jun 1997	62	12 825	Oct 1996	62
641 068	Mar 1998	63	12 825	Oct 1996	63

Table 3 – AIDS cases in the RSA compared with United States (*continued*)

United States	Surveillance Report Date		Ref	Republic of South Africa	Surveillance Report Date		Ref
691 647	Aug	1998	[64]	12 825	Oct	1996	[64]
717 430	Nov	1999	[65]	12 825	Oct	1996	[65]
733 374	Dec	1999	[66]	12 825	Oct	1996	[66]
806 157	Nov	2001	[67]	12 825	Oct	1996	[67]
859 000	Dec	2002	[68]	12 825	Oct	1996	[69]

Listed figures represent cumulative AIDS cases

3.2. AIDS Cases in All of Africa compared with United States

Along with the Republic of South Africa, all of Sub-Saharan Africa was purported to have devastating rates of HIV infection and consequent deaths. For example, the WHO/UNAIDS Sub-Saharan estimates for people living with HIV/AIDS (PLWH) increased from 7,500,000 people in 1993 to 28,000,000 in 2001.[67, 70]

Table 4 compares the number of reported AIDS cases in (all of) Africa with the number of reported AIDS cases in the United States for the years 1981–2002. Within Africa, each nation surveyed utilizing its own protocol. In Table 4, reported figures for "Africa" include surveillance data from cooperating nations in both Saharan and Sub-Saharan Africa.

One factor missing from this surveillance data are the *per capita* ratings of AIDS cases. For example, in 1999, the United States had 717,430 cumulative reported AIDS cases while all of Africa had 794,444 reported AIDS cases. These numbers indicate that the United States had an AIDS rate of 259 AIDS cases per 100,000 people while Africa had an AIDS rate of 103 AIDS cases per 100,000 people, using 1999 population statistics.[65, 71]

Table 4 – AIDS cases in all of Africa compared with United States

United States	Surveillance Report Date		Ref	All of Africa	Surveillance Report Date		Ref
5	Jun	1981	[21]				
355	Jun	1982	[72]				
1 641	Jun	1983	[25]				
4 918	Jun	1984	[26]				
10 000	Apr	1985	[27]				
29 003	Dec	1986	[29]				
40 845	Aug	1987	[30]				
48 139	Feb	1987	[73]	8 628	Feb	1988	[73]
55 167	Mar	1988	[32]	10 943	Apr	1988	[32]
57 575	Mar	1988	[74]	10 543	Jun	1988	[74]
65 099	Jun	1988	[33]	11 697	Aug	1988	[33]
78 985	Nov	1988	[34]	20 700	Jan	1989	[34]
80 538	Dec	1988	[35]	20 788	Feb	1989	[35]
84 503	Jan	1989	[36]	21 086	Mar	1989	[36]
86 656	Feb	1989	[37]	23 048	May	1989	[37]
92 719	May	1989	[38]	24 528	Jun	1989	[38]
95 561	May	1989	[39]	29 906	Aug	1989	[39]
98 255	Jun	1989	[40]	30 082	Sep	1989	[40]
100 885	Aug	1989	[41]	30 978	Oct	1989	[41]
104 210	Aug	1989	[42]	31 329	Nov	1989	[42]
107 308	Oct	1989	[43]	31 879	Dec	1989	[43]
113 211	Dec	1989	[44]	32 248	Jan	1990	[44]
117 781	Dec	1989	[45]	40 519	Feb	1990	[45]
126 127	Apr	1990	[46]	63 842	May	1990	[46]
137 385	Jul	1990	[47]	66 978	Aug	1990	[47]
140 822	Jul	1990	[48]	71 078	Sep	1990	[48]
144 221	Aug	1990	[49]	71 572	Oct	1990	[49]
149 498	Sep	1990	[50]	75 642	Nov	1990	[50]
171 876	Mar	1991	[51]	91 146	May	1991	[51]
202 843	Nov	1991	[52]	128 270	Feb	1992	[52]
242 146	Dec	1992	[53]	211 032	Jan	1993	[53]
289 320	Mar	1993	[54]	247 577	Jul	1993	[54]
339 250	Sep	1993	[55]	301 861	Jan	1994	[55]
411 907	Dec	1993	[56]	331 376	Jul	1994	[56]
401 789	Sep	1994	[57]	347 713	Jan	1995	[57]
441 528	Dec	1994	[58]	418 051	Jul	1995	[58]
501 310	Oct	1995	[59]	442 735	Dec	1995	[59]
513 486	Dec	1995	[60]	499 037	Jul	1996	[60]
565 097	Sep	1996	[61]	553 291	Nov	1996	[61]
581 429	Dec	1996	[17]	576 972	Jul	1997	[17]
612 078	Jun	1997	[62]	617 463	Nov	1997	[62]
641 068	Mar	1998	[63]	686 256	Jun	1998	[63]

Table 4 – AIDS cases in all of Africa compared with United States (*continued*)

United States	Surveillance Report Date	Ref	All of Africa	Surveillance Report Date	Ref
691 647	Aug 1998	[64]	706 318	Nov 1998	[64]
717 430	Nov 1999	[65]	794 444	Nov 1999	[65]
733 374	Dec 1999	[66]	876 009	Nov 2000	[66]
806 157	Oct 2001	[67]	1 093 522	Dec 2001	[67]
859 000	Dec 2002	[68]	1 111 663	Dec 2002	[75]

Listed figures represent cumulative AIDS cases
Listed figures for Africa include Saharan and Sub-Saharan Africa

Historically, some authors have proposed that some of the national surveillance data listed in Table 4 were inflated by the use of the WHO provisional surveillance definition for HIV/AIDS in national surveillance systems.[76-80] In some regions of Africa, excluding elite urban hospital settings, the standard mechanism for diagnosing and reporting AIDS was the provisional surveillance definition. This diagnostic algorithm was designed by WHO specifically for use in medical settings that lacked laboratory facilities for detecting HIV antibody or immunological dysfunction[*]; possibly contributing to the misdiagnosis of other chronic diseases as HIV/AIDS; such hypothetical misdiagnoses might be responsible, in part, for the atypical clinical profile of African HIV/AIDS patients which differs substantially from the presentation of HIV infection in American and European AIDS patients.[**] ("Clinical" in this book means "as seen in the doctor's office.")

In the Republic of South Africa, the HIV assay is now applied within the clinical diagnostic algorithm for HIV infection. For reasons described in brief below, the use of these diagnostic assays in the current diagnostic algorithm for HIV infection among tropical, indigent populations appears inappropriate.

---

[*] such dysfunction typically revealed by measurements of T4-cell count, T8-cell count, and T4/T8 cell ratio
[**] fully described and referenced in *HIV/AIDS – The Facts and the Fiction*, Health Alert Communications

3.3. WHO Estimates for all of Africa compared with Surveillance Data

In 1993, WHO started regularly publishing estimates for HIV/AIDS by global region along with reported surveillance data. The definitions of populations changed over time. Therefore, Table 5 compares the upper WHO estimates for HIV/AIDS in all of Africa with surveillance data from comparable time frames, where possible.

In Table 5, the Multiplication Factor shows the multiplicative relationship between the surveillance data and the estimates. For example, in 1992, Africa had reported 211,032 cumulative AIDS cases and the WHO estimate for Sub-African cases was 7,500,000; therefore the estimate was 35.5 times greater than the number of reported surveillance cases.

Table 5 – Sub-Saharan HIV/AIDS Estimates vs Cumulative Surveillance Data for All of Africa

WHO Estimates for Sub-Saharan Africa	Ref	Cumulative Surveillance Data for All of Africa	Surveillance Report Date	Ref	Multiplication Factor
7 500 000*	[70]	211 032	Jan 1993	[53]	35.5
8 000 000*	[81]	247 577	Jul 1993	[54]	32.3
7 000 000+	[82]	301 861	Jan 1994	[55]	23.2
8 000 000+	[83]	331 376	Jul 1994	[56]	24.1
8 000 000+	[57]	347 713	Jan 1995	[84]	23.0
8 500 000+	[85]	418 051	Jul 1995	[58]	20.3
14 000 000+	[86]	499 037	Jul 1996	[60]	28.1
14 000 000+	[87]	553 291	Nov 1996	[61]	25.3
20 800 000^	[88]	617 463	Nov 1997	[62]	33.6
20 800 000^	[63]	686 256	Jun 1998	[63]	30.3
22 500 000^	[64]	706 318	Nov 1998	[64]	31.9
23 300 000^	[65]	794 444	Nov 1999	[65]	29.0
25 300 000^	[66]	876 009	Nov 2000	[66]	28.8
28 100 000	[67]	—	Dec 2001	[67]	—
—	—	1 111 663	Dec 2002	[75]	—
25 400 000	[89]	—	Dec 2004	[89]	—
22 500 000	[10]	—	Dec 2007	[10]	—

Listed surveillance data represent cumulative AIDS cases including both Saharan and Sub-Saharan Africa

* 1993   Estimated cumulative total **adult AIDS cases/HIV infections** from late 1970s/early 1980s to date

+ 1994 – 1996   Estimated distribution of **adults living with HIV/AIDS** at specified date

^ 1997 – 2000   Estimated number of **adults and children living with HIV/AIDS** at specified date

Figure 1 – HIV/AIDS prevalence map, 2001 (WHO)

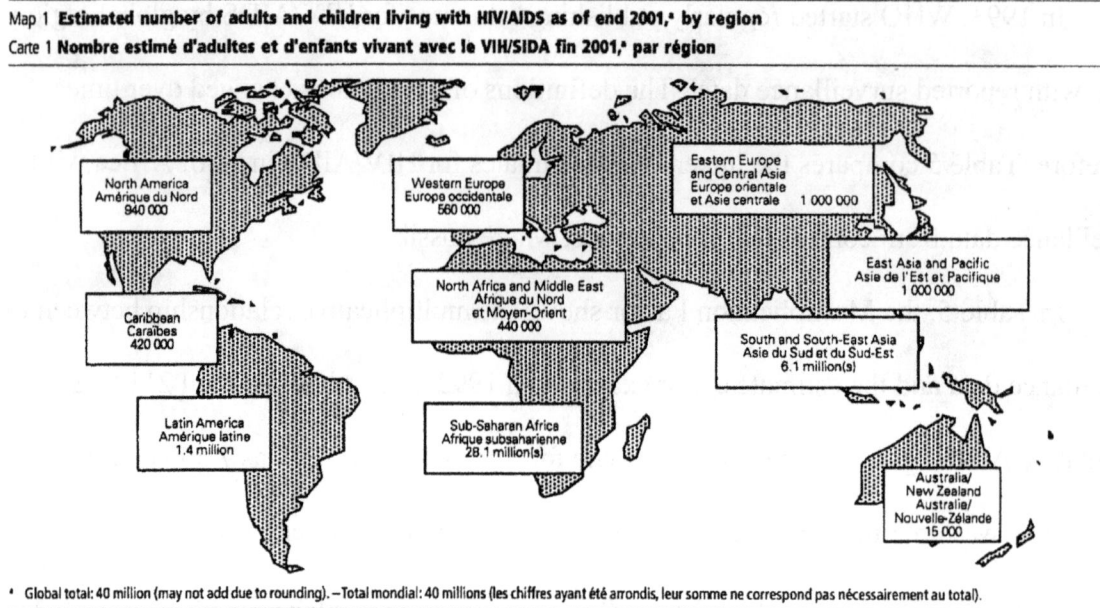

Map 1 **Estimated number of adults and children living with HIV/AIDS as of end 2001,ᵃ by region**
Carte 1 **Nombre estimé d'adultes et d'enfants vivant avec le VIH/SIDA fin 2001,ᵃ par région**

North America
Amérique du Nord
940 000

Western Europe
Europe occidentale
560 000

Eastern Europe
and Central Asia
Europe orientale
et Asie centrale   1 000 000

East Asia and Pacific
Asie de l'Est et Pacifique
1 000 000

Caribbean
Caraïbes
420 000

North Africa and Middle East
Afrique du Nord
et Moyen-Orient
440 000

South and South-East Asia
Asie du Sud et du Sud-Est
6.1 million(s)

Latin America
Amérique latine
1.4 million

Sub-Saharan Africa
Afrique subsaharienne
28.1 million(s)

Australia/
New Zealand
Australie/
Nouvelle-Zélande
15 000

* Global total: 40 million (may not add due to rounding). – Total mondial: 40 millions (les chiffres ayant été arrondis, leur somme ne correspond pas nécessairement au total).

Source: WHO. Global situation of the HIV/AIDS pandemic, end 2001. Part I. *Wkly Epidemiol Rec.* Dec 7 2001; 76 (49):381-386.

Figure 2 – HIV/AIDS prevalence map, 2004 (WHO)

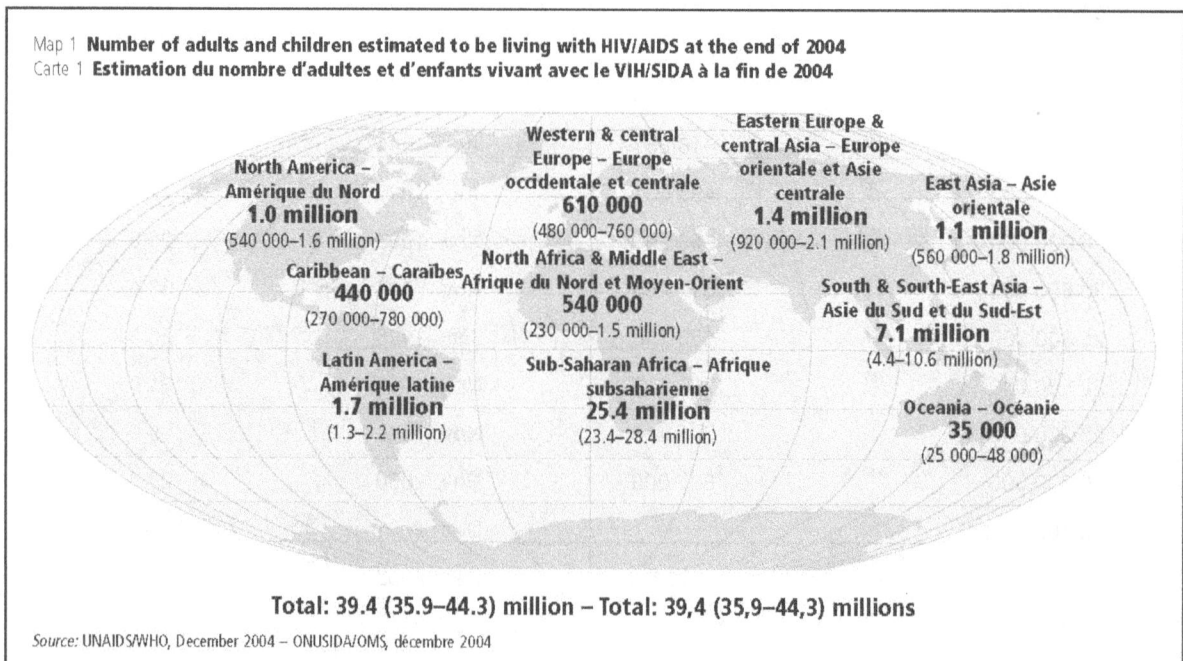

Map 1 **Number of adults and children estimated to be living with HIV/AIDS at the end of 2004**
Carte 1 **Estimation du nombre d'adultes et d'enfants vivant avec le VIH/SIDA à la fin de 2004**

North America –
Amérique du Nord
1.0 million
(540 000–1.6 million)

Western & central
Europe – Europe
occidentale et centrale
610 000
(480 000–760 000)

Eastern Europe &
central Asia – Europe
orientale et Asie
centrale
1.4 million
(920 000–2.1 million)

East Asia – Asie
orientale
1.1 million
(560 000–1.8 million)

Caribbean – Caraïbes
440 000
(270 000–780 000)

North Africa & Middle East –
Afrique du Nord et Moyen-Orient
540 000
(230 000–1.5 million)

South & South-East Asia –
Asie du Sud et du Sud-Est
7.1 million
(4.4–10.6 million)

Latin America –
Amérique latine
1.7 million
(1.3–2.2 million)

Sub-Saharan Africa – Afrique
subsaharienne
25.4 million
(23.4–28.4 million)

Oceania – Océanie
35 000
(25 000–48 000)

Total: 39.4 (35.9–44.3) million – Total: 39,4 (35,9–44,3) millions

Source: UNAIDS/WHO, December 2004 – ONUSIDA/OMS, décembre 2004

Source: WHO. Global situation of the HIV/ AIDS epidemic, end 2004. *Wkly Epidemiol Rec.* Dec 10 2004; 79 (50):441-449.

Figure 3 – HIV/AIDS prevalence map, 2007 (UNAIDS/WHO)

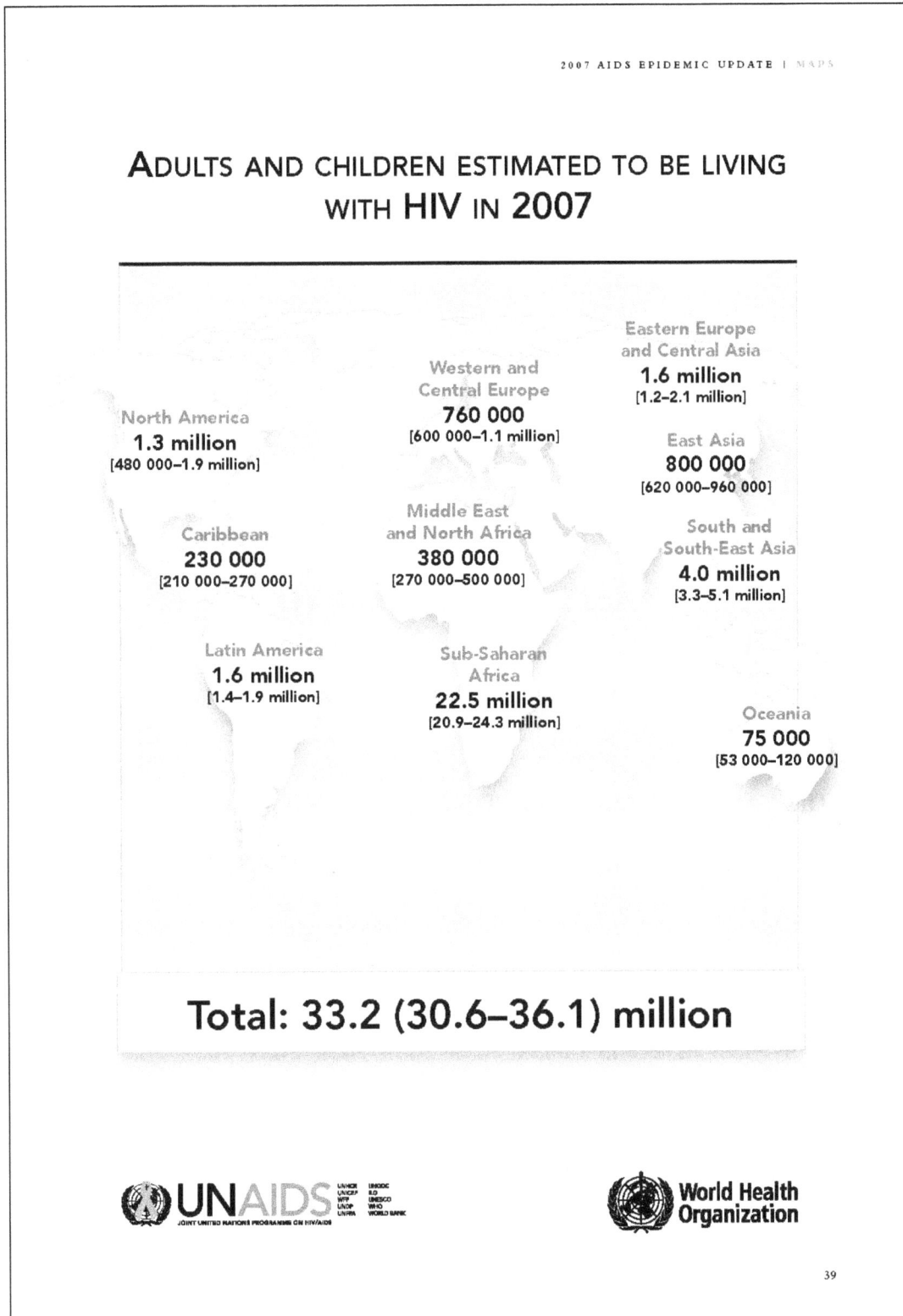

ADULTS AND CHILDREN ESTIMATED TO BE LIVING
WITH HIV IN 2007

North America
1.3 million
[480 000–1.9 million]

Western and
Central Europe
760 000
[600 000–1.1 million]

Eastern Europe
and Central Asia
1.6 million
[1.2–2.1 million]

East Asia
800 000
[620 000–960 000]

Caribbean
230 000
[210 000–270 000]

Middle East
and North Africa
380 000
[270 000–500 000]

South and
South-East Asia
4.0 million
[3.3–5.1 million]

Latin America
1.6 million
[1.4–1.9 million]

Sub-Saharan
Africa
22.5 million
[20.9–24.3 million]

Oceania
75 000
[53 000–120 000]

Total: 33.2 (30.6–36.1) million

UNAIDS
JOINT UNITED NATIONS PROGRAMME ON HIV/AIDS

World Health
Organization

39

Source: UNAIDS/WHO. *AIDS epidemic update: December 2007.* Geneva, Switzerland December 2007.
UNAIDS/07.27E / JC1322E.

Figure 4 – HIV/AIDS prevalence slide, 2002 (UNAIDS/WHO)

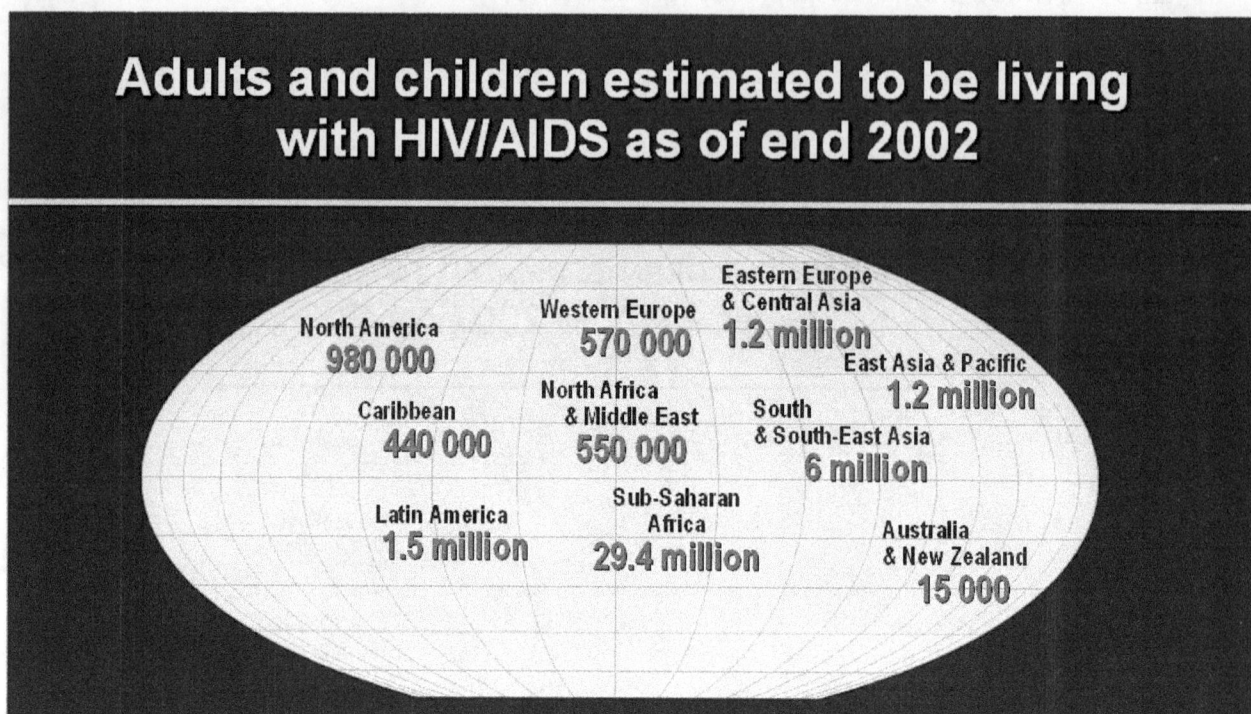

Source: http://www.who.int/hiv/strategic/en/epi_2002en.ppt (Accessed 29 Jul 2011)

3.4. The Search for More HIV/AIDS Deaths in the RSA

Overall, Statistics South Africa believes in the validity of the UNAIDS statistics, and applies similar statistical models and underlying assumptions to develop its own internal estimates.[16, 90] Therefore, RSA's Department of Health (**DOH**) publishes *estimates* similar to those of WHO/UNAIDS, as seen in Table 6.

As seen in Table 2 (Chapter 2), only 2.0% – 2.5% of all deaths were attributed to HIV/AIDS deaths per the death notification tabulations between 1997 and 2008.[2, 7, 9, 11-13] Statistics South Africa assumes the other deaths, approximately 35% to 40% of HIV/AIDS deaths, are hidden. First, Statistics South Africa believes HIV/AIDS cases are not being reported. Statistics South Africa presumes that "people don't want to disadvantage their family" and/or "lose their life insurance." Therefore, cooperative private physicians presumably write down the "immediate cause" of death on the death notification form (such as "pneumonia" instead of "AIDS"), and/or the patient refuses the voluntary, free HIV antibody test available at 3077 public clinics and 313 community health centers distributed throughout the RSA.[*]

Table 6 – RSA/DOH Estimates for Births, Deaths, and PLWH, 2001–2010

	Number of births	Total number of deaths	Estimated Total number of AIDS deaths	Percentage AIDS deaths (%)	Total number of people living with HIV (in millions)
2001	1 142 909	526 052	198 030	37,6	4,10
2002	1 140 844	569 535	236 390	41,5	4,38
2003	1 136 390	609 562	271 488	44,5	4,53
2004	1 129 598	645 371	302 530	46,9	4,64
2005	1 121 455	661 664	314 196	47,5	4,74
2006	1 113 087	666 473	314 309	47,2	4,85
2007	1 101 612	662 969	306 154	46,2	4,93
2008	1 089 916	646 187	284 658	44,1	5,02
2009	1 078 767	637 301	270 107	42,1	5,11
2010	1 066 401	654 360	281 404	43,0	5,24

Source: Table 4, HIV prevalence estimates and the number of people living with HIV, 2001–2010; Table 8, Births and deaths for the period 2001–2010; *Mid-year population estimates 2010.* In: Africa SS, ed. Pretoria, South Africa; 2010

Second, Statistics South Africa believes that a number of HIV/AIDS deaths are being miscoded. Per Statistics South Africa: "It is clear that many HIV deaths are not attributed to HIV on the death notification forms."[16] Therefore, Statistics South Africa seeks to find the "missing" AIDS deaths. One assumption is that many HIV/AIDS deaths are attributed to *parasitic infections.*[16] Parasitic infections increased between 1997 and 2004, mainly because of 4 parasitic infections (*candidiasis, cryptococcosis, toxoplasmosis* and *pneumocytosis*),[16] all diseases indicative of HIV infection. (However, these 4 parasitic opportunistic infections only accounted for 16% of all parasitic infections; malaria accounted for 86% of the remaining deaths from parasitic diseases in 2004.)[16] Other possible disease code misclassifications might have been: *all infectious diseases; certain disorders of the immune mechanism; tuberculosis; malaria;*

[*] Personal communication with Statistics South Africa

nutritional deficiencies; and certain *maternal conditions*.[16]

Statistics South Africa also states, "many of our thoughts agree with the causes that Groenewald *et al.* highlighted [for hidden HIV deaths]."[16] Groenewald *et al.* are a group of researchers at the Burden of Disease Research Unit, Biostatistics Unit, Medical Research Council of South Africa.[91, 92]

Groenewald *et al.* suggested that mortality statistics for South Africa under-reported HIV/AIDS deaths because of the "strict automated mechanistic coding practice" that Statistics South Africa utilized in generating its annual reports.[92] The first mortality report published by Statistics South Africa in 2005 contained death notification data for the years 1997 – 2003. Prior to issuing this final report, Statistics South Africa had generated an interim report using only 12% of the available data.[93] This interim report had been generated by hand: health professionals reviewed the listed *cause of death* on the death notification documents and assigned the disease classification code. In this interim report, HIV disease was attributed as the *underlying cause of death* for 8.7% of all deaths compared with 2.0% – 2.5% in the final report.[2, 7, 9, 11-13, 92, 93]

Groenewald *et al.* concluded that a "substantial number of deaths that were actually due to HIV" were misclassified as "*tuberculosis, lower respiratory infections, diarrhoeal diseases, bacterial meningitis, other respiratory disease, non-infective gastroenteritis, other infectious and parasitic disease, deficiency anaemias,* and *protein energy malnutrition*" and *Kaposi's sarcoma*.[16, 91]

Furthermore, Groenewald *et al.* concluded that 8% of all HIV/AIDS deaths in 2002 were recorded as such, which translates into 26% of all 2002 RSA deaths being HIV/AIDS deaths.[91, 92]

Statistics South Africa also cites Birnbaum et al., a group of researchers from the Institute for Health Metrics and Evaluation, University of Washington. Birnbaum et al. concluded that many HIV/AIDS deaths had been misclassified as: *tuberculosis; sexually transmitted diseases excluding HIV infection; intestinal infectious diseases; selected vaccine-preventable diseases;*

parasitic and vector-borne diseases; meningitis and encephalitis; respiratory infections; other

infectious diseases; maternal conditions; nutritional deficiencies; endocrine, nutritional, blood,

and immune disorders; non-communicable respiratory diseases; other digestive diseases; and

"garbage" codes.[94] Given the worst case scenario of the Birnbaum analysis, 48% of all RSA

deaths were actually HIV/AIDS deaths between 1996 and 2006.[94]

Table 7 attempts to place all these estimates into perspective relative to the RSA death

counts. Therefore, for the Republic of South Africa, Table 7 lists by year:

- UNAIDS estimates for people living with HIV/AIDS (PLWH);
- UNAIDS estimates for HIV/AIDS deaths;
- HIV/AIDS deaths per RSA death notifications
- All deaths per RSA death notifications
- HIV/AIDS deaths as 8.7% of all deaths (per Groenewald)[91, 92]
- HIV/AIDS deaths as 26% of all deaths (per Groenewald)[91, 92]; and
- HIV/AIDS deaths as 48% of all deaths (per Birnbaum).[94]

In addition, the Author of this book added one column entitled *Anticipated HIV/AIDS*

Deaths Within 4 Years Given Legitimate PLWH Estimate. Given the Author's understanding of

the HIV/AIDS infection via the medical literature, this column lists the estimated number of

HIV/AIDS deaths that should have occurred, had the WHO estimates for the number of people

living with HIV/AIDS represented legitimate HIV infections. The Author's reasoning is

summarized at the end of Section 5.2.3, *HIV/AIDS Mortality in Untreated Patients*.

Table 7 – Models for estimating RSA AIDS Deaths vs. RSA Death Notifications

Year	UNAIDS Estimates		Anticipated HIV/AIDS Deaths within 4 Years	RSA Death Notifications		Alternate Models*		
	Living with HIV/AIDS	HIV/AIDS Deaths	Given Legitimate PLWH Estimate	HIV/AIDS Deaths	All Deaths	HIV is 8.7% of all RSA Deaths	HIV is 26% of all RSA Deaths	HIV is 48% of all RSA Deaths
1997	2 900 000	140 000	1 100 000	6 235	317 132	27,590	82,454	152,223
1998	–	–	–	7 269	365 853	31,829	95,121	175,609
1999	4 200 000	250 000	1 600 000	9 935	381 820	33,218	99,273	183,273
2000	–	–	–	10 459	416 155	36,205	108,200	199,754
2001	4 600 000 – 5 000 000	180 000 – 360 000	1 700 000 – 1 900 000	9 244	454 882	39,574	118,269	218,343
2002	–	–	–	10 491	502 050	43,678	131 137	240,984
2003	–	–	–	11 650	556 779	48,439	144,762	267,253
2004	–	–	–	13 319	576 709	50,173	149 944	276,820
2005	–	–	–	14 532	598 131	52,037	155,514	287,102
2006	–	–	–	14 783	612 778	53,311	159 322	294,133
2007	5 700 000	350 000	2 100 000	13 521	603 094	52,469	156,804	289,485
2008	5 300 000	–	2 000 000	15 097	–	–	–	–
2009	5 600 000	310 000	2 100 000	–	–	–	–	–

See Tables 1 and 2 for references on UNAIDS estimates and RSA death notifications.

* The estimated number of HIV/AIDS deaths that should have occurred, in the Author's opinion, if the WHO estimates for the number of people living with HIV/AIDS had represented legitimate HIV infections. An explanation of the Author's reasoning is presented in Section 5.2.3.

4. THE FIRST AIDS CASES IN THE RSA

The first two documented AIDS cases in South Africa occurred with two gay men – both flight stewards who had visited the United States. The first man fell ill in early 1982. He had traveled regularly to the USA in course of duty, and also had lived in New York City for 5 years. The second man was a sexual partner of the first man, and also had visited the USA 3 to 4 months prior to the onset of illness. Both died within a year of illness onset.[23, 24]

Both of these AIDS cases occurred very early in the epidemic – less than 1 year after the U.S. Centers for Disease Control (CDC) became aware of AIDS and began counting cases.[21]

Three years later (1985), serum samples from 843 South Africans, Kenyans, and Namibians were tested for HIV antibodies. By this time, there had been several published reports of AIDS among Black Africans. The first Africans reported to have AIDS were residents of Belgium, but there we also reports from Africa. The majority of the AIDS cases reported among Africans in both locales were Francophones, native French-speaking African.* Several authors had also suggested that the yet-undetermined causative agent of AIDS might be endemic in Africa.[95-98] Scientists at South Africa's National Institute of Virology (NIV) had conducted seroprevalence studies with these concepts "in mind."[99] They used an **indirect immunofluorescence assay** in a laboratory; i.e., commercial HIV antibody tests were not yet available.* Table 8 lists the outcomes of this sero-survey.

Out of 843 people tested for the HIV antibody, only 35 gay men in Johannesburg, South Africa tested positive. Twelve of these gay men had AIDS. The remaining twenty-three gay men had AIDS prodrome, defined as chronic lymphadenopathy syndrome. An additional 4 patients with apparent AIDS prodrome tested negative. (The **AIDS prodrome** is the indeterminate period of vague malaise prior to the clinical presentation of opportunistic

---

* In this assay, antibodies marked with a fluorescent dye; the antibodies bind to viral antigens, and the marked antibodies are viewed via light microscopy. See *HIV/AIDS – The Facts and The Fiction* for detailed descriptions of HIV antibody testing issues and methodologies.

infections.) The majority of these men had visited the United States or had homosexual contact with a man who had visited the United States.[99]

Table 8 – African Populations tested in 1985 for HIV (*n* = 843)

Test Result	Description	Race	Location
Negative	143 Adults	Black	Namibia/South West Africa
Negative	139 Adults	Black	Kenya
Negative	51 NIV staff	Black	Johannesburg, South Africa
Negative	67 Nurses	Black	Johannesburg, South Africa
Negative	96 Two-year olds	Black	Johannesburg, South Africa
Negative	75 Renal transplant patients	Black/White	Johannesburg, South Africa
Negative	50 Institutionalized children	White	Johannesburg, South Africa
Negative	49 NIV staff	White	Johannesburg, South Africa
Negative	76 Nurses	White	Johannesburg, South Africa
Negative	58 Lymphoma patients	White	Johannesburg, South Africa
Positive	*12 Gay men with AIDS*	*White*	*Johannesburg, South Africa*
Positive	*23 Gay men AIDS prodrome*	*White*	*Johannesburg, South Africa*
Negative	*4 Gay men AIDS prodrome*	*White*	*Johannesburg, South Africa*

In comparison to these 35 White, South African, seropositive, gay men with AIDS or AIDS prodrome, the United States had a total of 10,000 AIDS cases at that time (May 1985).[27]

Regarding the migration of HIV from New York City to South Africa via air stewards, the story repeated itself several years later in Cape Town. As late as 1985, the appearance two HIV/AIDS cases in Cape Town, South Africa was still worthy of publication in the *South African Medical Journal*. The first AIDS patient in Cape Town was air steward who had lived in NYC. The second Cape Town AIDS patient was a sexual partner of the first patient. The two had lived together for 5 years.[100]

According to the authors if this journal article, at the time this journal article was composed, South Africa had "at least 18 cases of AIDS." Comparatively, the United States had 9,608 cases.

Approximately one year later, South Africa had 30 cases of AIDS (October 1986) while the United States had 29,003 cases (December 1986).[28, 29, 101]

Even given the small number of patients, the association of AIDS with America was fairly clear: "In South Africa, direct or indirect contact with a North American homosexual man is usually found in [South African] AIDS patients who have acted as the passive partner." [241]

The incipient pattern of AIDS cases in the Republic of South Africa (RSA) was the same pattern seen in Denmark, West Germany, England, France, Haiti, and the Caribbean island nations.* The majority of the AIDS patients in the RSA were homosexual men who had sexual contact with gay men in the United States or Europe.[24] Later, this pattern of transmission changed and the virus began to spread among South African homosexual men.[24]

"By the end of March 1987, 64 cases of AIDS had been treated in South Africa, 50 of them South Africans. All the South Africans were White males from the high risk groups characteristically seen in Western countries."[102] Comparatively, three months earlier (December 1986) the United States had accumulated 29,003 AIDS cases.[29]

In 1983, a survey of 250 RSA gay men reported 48% (12/25) as having 20 different sexual partners in the preceding 12 months.[24] Or . . . about half the level of sexual activity self-reported by gay men in the New York City vicinity. Prior to the advent of AIDS, NYC gay males were surveyed as averaging 20 sex partners in a 6-month period, or approximately 1000 sexual partners in a life time.[103-105]

The advent of AIDS in the RSA reflected a second pattern of international HIV transmission seen previously. In the RSA, Scotland, and Denmark, HIV was imported into the country via American blood products, namely plasma-derived clotting factors for the treatment of hemophilia.* In the RSA, 85% of hemophiliacs in the RSA treated with Factor VIII, imported from the United States, were seropositive for the HIV antibody (55/66) compared with 3% of hemophiliacs treated with local RSA product (3/98). (The American products were from large

---

* described and referenced in *HIV/AIDS – The Facts and the Fiction*, Health Alert Communications
* the circumstances in Scotland and Denmark are described and referenced in *HIV/AIDS – The Facts and the Fiction*, Health Alert Communications

donor pools and the local products from small donor pools; on average, patients received similar amounts Factor VIII per annum.) [106]

A concern with HIV/AIDS among the African Black population of the RSA was raised by a researcher in October 1989. At that time, the RSA had 166 AIDS cases. Of these 166 cases, 152 were male.[24] However, there was a ". . . most alarming development . . . the marked increase of cases in the Black population from 5 in 1987 to 17 in 1988."[24] The researcher concluded: "HIV infection and AIDS in South Africa have so far followed the pattern seen in Western countries . . . [there has been an] alarming increase in number of AIDS cases and HIV-positive people in the Black community. If this trend continues can anticipate an "African-type" HIV pattern in South Africa in near future."[24] (In October 1989, the RSA had 166 AIDS cases and the United States had 110,868 cases.[107, 108])

By "African-type" HIV pattern, the researcher is referring to reports of AIDS having originated and being endemic in "central Africa." "Central Africa" generally refers to the Republic of the Congo (formerly known as Zaire), which years earlier had received international acclaim in the public and scientific media for its reputed HIV endemicity. The first author to report AIDS among Africans in Africa (and not Europe) was Peter Piot, PhD, who identified 38 apparent AIDS cases in Kinshasa, Zaire in 1983, before HIV's discovery.[97] Piot eventually became Executive Director of the Joint United Nations Programme on HIV/AIDS (UNAIDS).

5. Why are the Estimates so Escalated?

Overall, the mathematical models are subject to two common misunderstandings of HIV infection. The first misunderstanding is that HIV has a median 8- to 11-year incubation period.[90, 109-115] (Relative to HIV/AIDS discussions, incubation period is generally conceived of as the time of initial infection until the development of opportunistic disease.)

The second misconception is that HIV antibody assays are accurate in all asymptomatic and/or symptomatic populations. A third adjoining misunderstanding is that HIV infection is a catch-all for all other infectious diseases.

5.1. Misconception of the HIV Incubation Period

Contrary to popular belief, HIV does not necessarily have a 10-year incubation period. **Incubation** is the period from initial infection until the onset of opportunistic disease (such as PCP, KS, or candidiasis).[*]

By March 1983, even before HIV was discovered, the CDC estimated that HIV infection had an 8- to 18-month incubation period.[116] AIDS was a mystery at outset, and health authorities had actively tracked and interviewed patients when possible to gather information both about possible etiology and transmission vectors (both unknown at that time). Not much of this empirical data was published in the medical literature and cohorts reported by CDC are very small, but in each cohort, a portion of the patients had short incubation periods.

As stated by the CDC: "Furthermore, the California cluster investigation and other epidemiologic findings suggest a 'latent period' of several months to 2 years between exposure and recognizable clinical illness and imply that transmissibility may precede recognizable illness."[117] Among infants born with HIV infection, the incubation period was typically 6 months or less, although a "failure to thrive" was sometimes immediately evident."[117-121] As of

---

[*] *Pneumocystis carinii* pneumonia (PCP), Kaposi's sarcoma (KS), and candidiasis – descriptions are forthcoming

1988, the median survival of infants born with HIV infection, or infected with HIV by transfusions, was 8 –9 months.[122]

The "California cluster" referred to by the CDC was a cluster of 19 gay men in California with PCP and/or KS: 7 alive and 11 dead. Of the 19 patients, sexual partner data was obtained for 13 patients. Within 5 years of symptom onset, 9 of these patients had had sexual contact with other KS of PCP patients. Three of the 6 patients with KS developed their symptoms after sexual contact with persons who already had symptoms of KS. One of these 3 patients developed symptoms of KS 9 months after sexual contact. Another patient developed symptoms 13 months after contact, and a third patient developed symptoms 22 months after contact.[123]

This evidence on incubation from this cohort of 19 is less conclusive than the Danish study, described below. It seems likely that these three patients, or any member of this cohort, may also have had one or more sexual contacts with men who were infected with HIV and **viremic** (the presence of viruses in the blood), but asymptomatic.

In one published study, the CDC had traced 40 AIDS patients linked by sexual contact to 10 cities. Based on 6 patients in this cohort, as determined by direct patient interview, the CDC estimated a mean latency period of 10.5 months. In these 6 patients, symptoms were first noticed a mean of 10.5 months (range 7 to 14 months) between sexual contact and symptom onset. The sexual contact was with one of four cohort members who also was a reported patient.[124]

Similar but more definitive findings were found in Denmark. In Denmark, AIDS first appeared among a cluster of homosexual men who had traveled to the United States. Eight of the first 20 AIDS patients in Denmark had visited the United States, which was then recognized as the epicenter of AIDS (New York, San Francisco, and Los Angeles, more precisely). To quote the authors: "Assuming that the travelers did contract the disease while in the USA, speculations about the incubation period might be relevant. The median period between departure from the USA and the diagnosis was 12 months (range 4 – 39) and the median period between arrival in the USA and the diagnosis was 25 months (range 6 – 41). Although our data indicate an average incubation period of 1-2 years, we cannot rule out the possibility that it may be even longer."[125] These Danish authors also reported a 6-month incubation period. The subject presented with opportunistic infection 6 months after sexual contact in the United States.[125]

One study among 10 cancer patients who had all received transfusions from a single, HIV-infected, blood donor also indicated a minimal incubation period of 1 – 2 years.[126] In all, 25 patients had received contaminated blood from a single donor; however, this study focused on the 10 patients still living at the time. Of these 10 patients, 9 were seropositive and 6 had clinical and/or immunological (laboratory) indications of HIV infection. Table 9 describes this small patient population.

Table 9 - Incubation Periods in 10 Cancer Patients infected via Transfusion

Patient No.	AIDS-Defining Condition	Days after Transfusion
2	*Pneumocystis carinii* pneumonia (PCP)	745
5	*Pneumocystis carinii* pneumonia (PCP)	411
7	*Pneumocystis carinii* pneumonia (PCP)	365
8	*Cryptococcal meningitis*	266
3	Thrombocytopenic	233
6	Thrombocytopenic	56

Both *Pneumocystis carinii* pneumonia (PCP) and cryptococcal meningitis are caused by fungal organisms and indicative of a defect in cell-mediated immunity (the type of immunodeficiency induced by HIV infection). **Thrombocytopenia** is the relative lack platelets in the blood; platelets being the blood components that assist in blood clotting. Patients with thrombocytopenia tend to bruise and/or bleed easily. Thrombocytopenia can be an AIDS-related condition.)

In these patients, the median incubation period was 286 days (9.5 months) (range 56 – 745 days), including the patients with thrombocytopenia. However, for the sake of argument, the Author discounts the 2 patients with thrombocytopenia. All these cancer patients were under medical observation; otherwise, such hematological (relating to the blood) indications of HIV infection might have passed unnoticed among the population at large, and might not have driven the average person to the doctor seeking medical care.

Thus, 4 of 10 patients developed clinically evident opportunistic infections within 266 – 745 days (9 months – 2 years) after HIV infection was introduced via blood transfusion.[126]

It must also be stated that cell-mediated immunity occurs among some patients with cancer. So it is possible that the underlying cancerous conditions of these patients also induced and/or contributed to the development of these opportunistic infections. Yet the apparent minimal HIV incubation period of 1 – 2 years among a subset of this population mirrors that of the cohorts described previously.

A few sporadic, shorter incubation periods have been reported:

- a 2-month incubation period following sexual contact in a homosexual male contact;[127]

- a 2-month incubation period, from intravenous needle transmission to the development of lymphadenopathy;[128] * and

- a 7-week incubation period to the development of AIDS-related complex following a blood transfusion.[129]

One author reported two short-term periods of progression from "primary infection" to

---

* **Lymphadenopathy** means "disease of the lymphatic system." The lymphatic system is the human body's second fluid system which contains a clear fluid called lymph. In the doctor's office, lymphadenopathy is the prolonged swelling of the glands – lymph nodes – in the neck, armpits, and groin. Lymphadenopathy may progress slowly or quickly to terminal AIDS.)

AIDS. A 32-year old homosexual male presented with a 4-day fever, abdominal pain, and diarrhea with blood. The author appears to assume this presentation was an acute reaction to an HIV infection that was acquired some weeks earlier (the author indicates he knows the time frame of exposure but does not describe it). Two weeks following this initial acute presentation, the patient developed lymphadenopathy, and then developed PCP (along with seroconversion to HIV positive) within 2 months of initial fever presentation.[130]

The same author reported a 73-year old woman who received 1 unit of blood. Two weeks after transfusion, she had acute illness with fever, malaise, weight loss, and lymphadenopathy which resolved without treatment after 8 weeks. She developed AIDS (seropositive plus cerebral toxoplasmosis) within 6 months after blood transfusion.[130]

These findings do not necessarily countermand the existence of individuals, or some portion of the HIV-infected population, that survive for 11 years without treatment or experience a silent 10-year incubation period. Yet in these virgin, untreated groups, 6 patients (among a network of 40 sexual contacts with AIDS) developed AIDS (manifested opportunistic infections) in a median 7.5 months after exposure (range 7 to 14 months), and 8/20 AIDS patients had average incubation periods of 1-2 years (range 4 to 39 months). The numbers in these available reports are very small, yet the incubation period they document likely represents the beginning edge of the distribution curve for HIV incubation.

Moreover, these first few cases heralded an incipient tsunami. For the first two years, the AIDS numbers in the United States doubled every 6 months.[22] By 1985, it had slowed to doubling every 12 months or so.[131, 132] By 1987 or so, the wave had crested, such that the annual prevalence increased only 4.9% from 1990 to 1991 (though the momentum of the threshold population continued to induce accumulation).[133]

Yet, in this time, humans were undergone a herd behavioral change. The gay bath houses closed and the culture dissipated; the gay discos had become Russian Roulette, and needle interventions were enacted via needle exchange and/or bleach. (And possibly, a significant proportion of those people at greatest risk had already died).

Also, during this time:

- the etiology of AIDS remained unsolved for 4 years;
- the CDC developed and distributed a surveillance definition based on utilizing clinical and immunological profiles;
- HIV was discovered and identified as the etiological agent;
- an HIV testing kit was developed and approved;
- modified CDC surveillance definitions were developed and distributed along with the establishment of an infrastructure for the purpose of distributing information to both clinicians and the general public;
- HIV/AIDS became mainstream news;
- a first-time ever human anti-retroviral drug was developed; and
- a radical political advocacy group named "ACT-UP!" was formed.

All these events occurred in less time than the purported median longevity of any particular HIV/AIDS patient, if one considers a 9 – 11 years (in developed countries) as median.

Incubation is discussed further in Section 5.2.4 (*Forgotten Knowledge*).

5.2. Misconception of the Natural Course for HIV Infection

5.2.1. THE T-CELL DEFECT

Contrary to some common perceptions, early stage HIV infection is not a catch-all for every infectious disease. The first blossoming opportunistic infections of untreated HIV infection are viral, fungal, and protozoal infections, because HIV kills off the T4-cell population, and the T4-cell triggers cellular immunity into action against viral, fungal, and protozoal infections.

To repeat, the T4-cell is the trigger for cellular immunity. ***Cellular immunity*** utilizes various distinct populations of white blood cells into action against an intruder. One such population is called the "natural killer cells," but basically all these cells attempt to engulf, disrupt, or destroy invaders. Cellular immunity is also known as ***cell-mediated immunity***.

The cellular defect induced by HIV infection (the failure of the T4-cell triggering mechanism) permits opportunistic viral, fungal, and protozoal infections and malignancies to grow unchecked. Effectively, these opportunistic infections can ravage the body and kill with extraordinary rapidity.

Although people with untreated HIV infections lose their cellular immunity, their humoral immunity remains intact and functional. **Humoral immunity** is the body's second blood-based immunological component: it utilizes antibodies to attack invaders. A certain type of white blood cell secretes antibodies into the bloodstream. Antibodies inactivate the invader by covering the surface of the invader, preventing the surface proteins of the invader from interacting with cellular proteins within the host. Antibodies also mark the invader for destruction by cellular killer cells.

During the early stages of HIV infection, patients still retain their humoral immunity; therefore, they maintain their immunological protection against bacterial infections. The presence of pathogenic bacterial infections is *not* evidence of HIV infections in absence of opportunistic viral, fungal, and protozoal infections. Infections by pathogenic bacteria are possible concurrent with HIV infection or independent of HIV infection.

Due to the debilitating nature of HIV/AIDS, many organs and metabolic systems can fall into failure, including humoral immunity. However, as a rule, such humoral impairment should develop in the later, debilitating stages of HIV infection. As a general rule, the initial blossoming opportunistic infections consequent to HIV should be viral, fungal, and protozoal.

Thus, in the opinion of this author, it is not necessarily appropriate to consider *all infectious diseases*, *non-communicable respiratory diseases*, *all sexually transmitted diseases*, *bacterial meningitis*, and *other infectious diseases* as possible disguised HIV infections, as done by Statistics South Africa and Birnbaum et al, mentioned above, in their attempts to identify the missing HIV/AIDS mortalities (and perhaps some of the other included codes as well).[16, 94] Groenewald also included *protein energy malnutrition*. Malnutrition, particularly, protein-malnutrition is known to impair cellular immunity, such that people with protein-malnutrition frequently manifest candidiasis due to this malnutrition-induced impairment of cell-mediated immunity. People with protein-malnutrition/malnutrition are also known to develop *Pneumocystis carinii* pneumonia (**PCP**), particularly infants.[134-141] Both candidiasis and PCP are typical presenting symptoms of HIV infection, but they can occur in protein-malnourished/malnourished people in absence of HIV infection. People with protein-malnutrition need not look gaunt.

5.2.2. Opportunistic Diseases consequent to the T-Cell Defect

Not all HIV-infected populations manifest the same opportunistic diseases. Populations manifest the diseases to which they are exposed.

In the United States, at the beginning of the AIDS epidemic, there were 2 primary *presenting symptoms* of HIV infection; that is, the first noticeable opportunistic infections. These infections were ***Pneumocystis carinii* pneumonia** (**PCP**) and Kaposi's sarcoma.[*] The manifestation of Kaposi's sarcoma subsequent to HIV infection evidently is caused by an uncontrolled viral infection; described in more detail below.[142-155]

At that time, people were said to have "AIDS" when they presented with opportunistic infections and/or Kaposi's sarcoma. (See the 1982 U.S. Centers for Disease Control case definition in Appendix E.) HIV had not yet been discovered; the cause of AIDS was unknown.

---

[*] *Pneumocystis carinii* has been renamed *Pneumocystis jiroveci*; the older term is used in this document

HIV was added to the case definition in 1985.[156] After the discovery of HIV, a classification system for HIV infection was developed.[157, 158] In this classification system, "AIDS" technically became the last stage of HIV infection.

In the United States, *Pneumocystis carinii* pneumonia (PCP) was the most common presenting symptom of HIV infection. PCP manifested in more than 50% of all AIDS patients before any other symptom appeared. Either alone or together with Kaposi's sarcoma, PCP was a presenting symptom in roughly 55% – 70% of all AIDS patients.[22, 25, 26, 159-166] In fact, AIDS first gained national attention because of 5 gay men hospitalized with PCP in Los Angeles.[21, 167] (However, the first likely legitimate case of AIDS-related *Pneumocystis carinii* was diagnosed in New York City 19 months before the first PCP case was diagnosed in Los Angeles.)[21, 167-169]

As seen in the United States, PCP was the classic, early onset, AIDS-related opportunistic infection, alone accounting for roughly half of AIDS deaths (43% to 58%) during the first years of the epidemic.[22, 159-162, 170] PCP was a swift killer and the primary cause of AIDS mortality. In the United States, among the first 159 AIDS patients, 40% died from their *initial* PCP infection.[171] In Britain, among the first 130 AIDS cases, mortality from the first attack of *Pneumocystis carinii* pneumonia (PCP) was about 33%.[172]

Kaposi's sarcoma was the second most common opportunistic infection in the United States. (**Kaposi's sarcoma** is a malignant skin cancer first appearing as pink, purple or brown lesions, usually on arms and/or legs, and then spreading around body and, in AIDS patients, perhaps inducing death by spreading to gastrointestinal tract, lungs, and other internal organs.) KS was almost an exclusively homosexual phenomenon, due to the sexual transmission of its etiological agent: the Kaposi's sarcoma herpes virus (KSHV). KSHV is also known as human herpes virus 8 (HHV-8), evidently transmitted by fecal contact. KSHV/HHV-8 is evidently spread during sexual activity involving fecal contact.[142-155] Kaposi's sarcoma was almost absent in all other American risk groups (IV drug users; hemophiliacs; transfusion and organ recipients, and male and female heterosexuals).[170, 173] The existence of a corresponding high prevalence of KS in the RSA seems unlikely. (The "natural" indolent form Kaposi's sarcoma that is unrelated to HIV infection is said to be endemic in Central Africa; it is different from the aggressive KS seen during HIV infection.)

However, given the T4-cell defect induced by HIV infection, one or another ambient opportunistic organism native to the RSA, or native to the bodies of South Africans, should flourish. For example, in the United States, the most common opportunistic infection actually was candidiasis. Candidiasis developed in more HIV/AIDS patients than even PCP, but since candidiasis did not kill patients quickly, it tended to pass unnoticed in light of the other on-going clinical emergencies. **Candidiasis** is a disease caused by *Candida albicans*, a fungus. Candida is normally a benign, non-pathogenic organism that normally lives in the skin, mouth, vagina, gastrointestinal tract of humans without causing any problems. (The impaired cellular immunity that arises from protein-malnutrition and/or iron deficiency may allow the manifestation of candidiasis in such malnourished people.)[134-139]

During early HIV infection, candidiasis tends to manifest in the mouth and throat. In the early years of the AIDS epidemic, candidiasis would eventually develop in approximately 80% of AIDS patients over the course of HIV infection.[174]

Assuredly, in the Republic of South Africa, *Pneumocystis carinii*, *Candida albicans*, or some other ambient viral, fungal, or protozoal disease would routinely afflict members of the HIV-infected population. Presumably, there would be a rhyme and reason to these manifestations. In all likelihood, as with the American and European patients, a set of predominant opportunistic infections would come to the forefront and account for most of the fatalities in a symptomatically repetitive and identifiable manner.

5.2.3. HIV/AIDS MORTALITY IN UNTREATED PATIENTS

This document describes two factors related to HIV/AIDS mortality: incubation and survival. Incubation is the period from initial infection until the onset of opportunistic disease (such as PCP, KS, or candidiasis). Patient survival is the time from the development of opportunistic infections to death. Generally, these two factors are conceptually melded into one – hence the general belief that people live with HIV infection for 10 years.

Currently, given appropriate diagnosis and medical treatment, a 10-year survival period from infection to opportunistic infections or death seems entirely feasible.

However, at the advent of AIDS, HIV had not been discovered, and there were no effective treatments for the opportunistic infections that killed AIDS patients rapidly. Prior to the emergence of HIV, all these opportunistic organisms had been benign– unable to inflict disease on to death under ordinary circumstances. Therefore, no pharmaceutical arsenal against them had ever been assembled.

From the onset of AIDS (~1981) until 1985 or so, no drugs could effectively reduce HIV/AIDS mortality. Therefore, the mortality rates of American AIDS patients in this time period represent the capability of HIV infection to induce death among untreated AIDS patients.

Beginning in 1985 or so, the use of prophylactic pentamidine by front-line physicians greatly reduced PCP-related mortality and increased patient longevity. Pentamidine was used both as a prophylactic regimen and to treat on-going infections. Pentamidine significantly improved survival rates of patients diagnosed with *Pneumocystis carinii* pneumonia after 1985 or so.[175, 176] In the United States, gay men diagnosed with PCP in 1990-1991 had one-tenth the risk of dying as those diagnosed in 1984-1985.[177]

Table 10 depicts the mortality rates of the first AIDS cohorts reported in the United States. The time periods listed under Outcomes represents survival after onset of illness.

Table 10 – Mortality Rates of the First AIDS Cohorts in the United States, 1981

Opportunistic Infection	# Patients	Location	Time Period	Outcomes
P. carinii pneumonia *	11 patients	New York City	Apr 1979 – Apr 1981	• 8/11 dead within 24 months
Anal *Herpes simplex* ulcers	4 gay men	New York City	Jul 1979 – Jul 1980	• 3/4 dead within 12 months
P. carinii pneumonia	4 gay men	Los Angeles	Feb 1981 – Apr 1981	• 2/4 dead within 3 months
Kaposi's sarcoma**	20 gay men	New York City	Jan 1979 – Jul 1981	• 7/20 dead within 24 months
	6 gay men	California		• 1/6 dead within 24 months

* Probably not all these patients had AIDS • 1 patient had terminal angioimmunoblastic lymphadenopathy with dysproteinemia (AILD) • others had questionable clinical profiles • overall cohort survival rate was atypically high • the majority were IV drug users; whereas, HIV had yet to enter the IV drug using population at large.

Source: Masur H, Michelis MA, Greene JB, et al. An outbreak of community-acquired Pneumocystis carinii pneumonia: initial manifestation of cellular immune dysfunction. N Engl J Med. Dec 10 1981;305(24):1431-1438 • Siegal FP, Lopez C, Hammer GS, et al. Severe acquired immunodeficiency in male homosexuals, manifested by chronic perianal ulcerative herpes simplex lesions. N Engl J Med. Dec 10 1981;305(24):1439-1444 • Gottlieb MS, Schroff R, Schanker HM, et al. Pneumocystis carinii pneumonia and mucosal candidiasis in previously healthy homosexual men: evidence of a new acquired cellular immunodeficiency. N Engl J Med. Dec 10 1981; 305 (24):1425-1431.

After PCP mortality was reduced, other opportunistic infections stepped forward to assume the mantle of dominant mortality. Eventually, most were wrestled into control with successful prophylactic and treatment regimens, extending the longevity of people infected with HIV. By the end of the 1980s, the use of antiretroviral drugs for HIV infection was becoming widespread. Around 1996, the use of highly active antiretroviral therapy versus HIV (HAART; the multiple drug cocktail) became widespread, further adding to life expectancy for PLWH.

Table 11 lists mortality rates for AIDS cohorts during June 1981 – May 1986 (the period before effective treatments and prophylaxis were available versus opportunistic infections). The percentages listed under Mortality Rates represent the percentage of patients who died after presenting opportunistic disease(s).

Table 11 – HIV/AIDS Mortality Rates 1981–1985, United States

Date Range	AIDS Cases	AIDS Deaths	Mortality Rates		Ref
Jun 1981 –Sept 1982	593	—	• Overall mortality	41%	22
			• PCP without KS*	47%	22
			• KS without PCP*	21%	22
			• Other opportunistic infection*	48%	22
Jun 1981 – Mar 1983	1,200+	450+	• Overall mortality	38%	117
			• Diagnosed > 1 year prior	60%	117
Jun 1981 – Aug 1983	1,972	759	• Overall mortality	38%	178
Jun 1981 – Dec 1984	7,699	3,665	• Overall mortality	48%	162
Jun 1981 – Dec 1985	15,948	8,161	• Overall mortality	51%	161
			• Mortality diagnosed before 1984	71%	101
Jun 1981 – May 1986	21,065	11,541	• Overall mortality	55%	179

* Percentage of patients who present this condition as the first manifestation of HIV infection

Table 12 lists survival rates among HIV/AIDS cohorts in developed countries. During much of this time, people were said to have "AIDS" when they presented with opportunistic infections and/or Kaposi's sarcoma (See the 1982 CDC case definition in Appendix E). These survival rates represent *the time of survival after the first manifestations of opportunistic infection(s)* and/or Kaposi's sarcoma. Such information does not address the length of HIV incubation, the time from infection until the manifestation of the first opportunistic infections, discussed previously.

It is worth noting that Table 12 describes two large populations in which only 2% to 5% of patients survived for 5 years after manifesting opportunistic disease ($n = 4,323$; $n = 12,020$).[122, 175]

Table 12 – HIV/AIDS Survival Rates among Cohorts in Developed Countries

Time Period	Location	Size of Cohort	Survival Rates	Ref
1981 – May 1983	San Francisco	75 90 90	**Median Survival:** • KS presentation – 21 months • PCP presentation – 9 months* • PCP presentation – 0% survival at 21 months	[180]
Jul 1981 – Dec 1988	San Francisco	4,323	**Median Survival:** • 12.5 months • Survival at 5 years – 3.4%	[175]
Jan 1984 –Sep 1987	United States	36,847	**PCP as first presentation:** • Estimated 1-yr survival – 42.7% (1981 – 1985) • Estimated 1-yr survival – 54.5% (1986 +)	[177]
Jan 1981 – Aug 1988	United States	716	**Median Survival of Hemophiliacs** • 6.4 months (1981 – 1985) • 15.0 months (1986 – 1988)	[181]
Jun 1984 – Jan 1992	Baltimore, Chicago, Los Angeles, and Pittsburgh	891	**Median survival:** • 11.6 months in 1984-1985 • 19.5 months in 1988-1989 • 17.2 months in 1990-1991	[176]
Literature Review, 1988	New York City New York State San Francisco UK & Italy	12,020+	**Median Survival:** • 9 – 13 months • Survival at 4 years – 2% to 5% **Transfusion Cases:** • Mean Incubation – 7.66 years. **Infants – Perinatal or Transfusion:** • Median Survival – 8 to 9 months	[122]

* Primarily *Pneumocystis carinii* pneumonia, but also other opportunistic infections

Accepting the 8- to 24-month incubation period identified by the Centers for Disease Control, then in any HIV/AIDS cohort, the first HIV/AIDS deaths should begin appearing approximately 20 months after the time HIV infection (the sum of an 8-month incubation plus a 12-month survival).[116, 117, 122-125, 177, 182] Also, in such an untreated cohort, only 2% to 5% should survive for 7 years post-infection (the sum of a 2-year incubation plus a 5-year survival).[122, 175]

Table 12, above, also highlights the PCP infection. Early in the epidemic, the median survival was 9 months after developing PCP.[180] The situation had improved by 1985-1987, but survival following its manifestation had increased by only 3 months. In this time period, roughly half of AIDS patients died within 12 months of developing PCP.[177]

In the Republic of South Africa (RSA), the first 2 AIDS patients (the two gay male flight stewards) both died from *Pneumocystis carinii pneumonia* (PCP) less than a year after becoming ill.[23, 24] Among the first 21 AIDS patients in the RSA, ten of them had PCP (48%).[28]

The causal agent of *Pneumocystis carinii* pneumonia is reportedly ubiquitous worldwide.[183, 184] One author cites a serological survey of Britain and Gambia showing 70% seroprevalence of antibodies to *Pneumocystis carinii* by eight years of age in both countries, similar to levels observed in the United States.[185-187] In the RSA, among HIV-infected patients and renal transplant patients receiving immunosuppressive drug therapy – both immunocompromised populations – the prevalence of PCP ranged from 22% to 43.7%.[188] PCP prevalence was also 10% – 50% among HIV-infected children ($n = 31$; $n = 105$; and $n = 151$), and 43% among South African HIV-infected adults ($n = 67$).[189]

Again, as seen in the United States, 38% of American AIDS patients died in the first 2 years of the AIDS epidemic (June 1981-August 1983). PCP was the classic, early onset, AIDS-related opportunistic infection. It was the most frequent presenting symptom, and PCP accounted for roughly half of AIDS deaths (43% to 58%) during the first years of the epidemic.[22, 159-162, 170] Therefore, in the Republic of South Africa, one should expect patient outcomes comparable with those observed initially in the United States.

Given 2,900,000 South Africans with HIV infection in 1998 (per WHO estimate), at least 1.1 million (38%) or so should have died by the end of 2002. The period from 1998 to 2002 is four years – allowing for a 2-year incubation period before the development of opportunistic infections. Once opportunistic diseases have appeared, approximately 38% of these AIDS patients should have died in the following 2-year period.

A 38% mortality rate is used in this example because this mortality rate was exhibited by the American HIV/AIDS epidemic in its initial 2 years.[178] It is also the lowest reported rate among a relatively large patient cohort ($n = 1,972$). (In all subsequent CDC reports, the mortality rate would be higher; therefore the use of 38% in this example is the most conservative approach.)

Presumably, the greater majority of these purported 2,900,000 PLWH had no access to the rather sophisticated prophylactic and/or antiretroviral regimens, nor to the sophisticated hospital facilities frequented by their American counterparts. Therefore, minimally, their mortality should have been comparable to untreated HIV/AIDS patients in the United States.

An underlying assumption is that *Pneumocystis carinii* would induce a substantial proportion of this 38% mortality, given evidence of PCPs presence in the South African environment.[23, 28, 188, 190, 191]

If not PCP, then some other ambient opportunistic viral, fungal, or protozoal organism(s) would have made themselves evident. Presumably, such prevailing opportunistic infections would not be haphazard. Rather, a repetitive *subset* of predominant conditions likely would emerge, owing to the presence of particular opportunistic organisms that reside in the ambient environment or in the body of the hosts. Or, such conditions would emerge because of potential host interaction with local transmission vectors. For example, in the United States, prior to the availability of effective prophylactic and/or treatment regimens, a subset of 3 initial presenting conditions occurred in approximately 70% of all AIDS patients; namely, PCP, KS, and/or candidiasis. Presumably, the course of any subset of opportunistic infections would likely be unchecked, rapidly terminal, repetitive, and as readily identifiable in the RSA as well.

Table, 7, contains a column entitled, *Anticipated HIV/AIDS Deaths within 4 Years Given Legitimate PLWH Estimate*. This column speculatively presents an anticipated HIV/AIDS death count by year, if the UNAIDS estimates for people living for AIDS represented legitimate HIV infections. These preceding paragraphs are the reasoning behind this speculative column.

5.2.4. FORGOTTEN KNOWLEDGE

The conception of longevity among HIV/AIDS patients changed over time. Initially, in absence of any knowledge concerning the emerging syndrome, investigators interviewed patients in attempts to determine the etiology, transmission vectors, and incubation period of this new, uncharacterized, deadly syndrome. Their efforts may provide the best empirical evidence on the nature of HIV incubation (at least among a subset of a larger HIV/AIDS cohort).

As the epidemic progressed, patients kept coming forward with longer incubation periods.[101, 192, 193] Once the scale of the epidemic moved beyond the feasibility of individual tracking and recording, investigators began modeling incubation, survival, and seroconversion rates among large, available cohorts of gay men. (**Seroconversion** is the change from a negative outcome to a positive, in the HIV antibody test.) In these models, the estimated incubation period consistently increased over time. However, these models are based only in part on raw data: they are also based on estimated and imputed values.[176, 194-201] (The number of these models proliferate far beyond the few cited here.) In these estimates, the shapes of the curves projecting 10-year incubation periods have been filtered through pre-selected distribution models. By way of example, one modeled estimate published in 1990 stated "[the] estimated incubation period hazard function is near zero for two years following infection,"[202] a statement contrary to the empirical evidence gathered by the CDC and others early in the epidemic.[116, 117, 123-125, 127-129, 182]

Investigations based on interviews with AIDS patients indicated that silent incubation in some subset of the AIDS population averaged 8 to 24 months. The numbers of patients represented in these investigations were small, but these were the investigative outcomes when the efforts of investigative epidemiologists were focused on tracking and interviewing individual AIDS patients. (Transfusion recipients seemed to have legitimately longer incubation periods than members of other high risk groups.) Excepting these initial reports, other incubation estimates are models. There is no large database of raw empirical data detailing incubation for hundreds or thousands of patients. Rather, the incubation periods imputed into the computer models are mathematical models themselves.[176, 194-201]

In 1984, HIV was accepted as the etiological cause of AIDS and virologists began discussing the other pathogenic retroviruses known at the time. Before HIV was theorized to come from African primates, retrovirus research focused on problematic retroviruses infecting economic farm animals (goats, sheep cattle, and horses).[203-211] Retroviruses, in general, were known to have long, silent incubation periods of unspecified length. [A retrovirus is a virus that encodes genetic information within RNA and utilizes a DNA intermediate during replication; that is, during the replication process, the RNA strand(s) within the retrovirus is reverse-transcribed ("reverse written") into DNA, and then this DNA intermediate is transcribed ("written") into RNA; the final RNA product is then inserted into viral replicas. Not all RNA-based viruses are retroviruses.]

Around 1985 or so, given the success of PCP prophylaxis in clinical trials, the medical community speculated that (with treatment) survival from time of infection might be extended to 10 years. This speculation was picked up and echoed extensively by the general and scientific media.

Thus, all these concepts melded into the belief that HIV infection in untreated patients had a silent 10-year incubation from the time of infection to manifestation of opportunistic infections, and/or HIV/AIDS patients survived for 10 years from the time of infection until the time of death.*

As the melded concept became a truism, some of the details were dropped. For example, the UNAIDS modelers state the median survival of HIV/AIDS patients in highly industrialized countries was approximately 11 years *before the advent of HAART*.[109] (The estimate for median

---

* Author's opinion of how this concept developed as a truism

survival in low- and middle-income countries was 9 years.[109, 112, 212])

The phrase "before the advent of HAART" does *not* mean entire absence of treatment. Prior to 1985, no effective drug treatments were available. After 1985, new effective drugs for treatment and/or prophylaxis became available, which extended the longevity of AIDS cohorts thereafter.[175-177, 213] The first antiretroviral drug was approved in 1987.[214] Several more soon followed. Initially they were administered singularly. All of these treatments successfully extended patient survival before HAART was introduced. (HAART implementation became widespread in 1996.[109]) Therefore, a survival period averaging 11 years for AIDS patients diagnosed after 1985 seems feasible, since they would have been receiving treatment. Moreover, any study of mortality rates, survival rates, and disease progression in HIV cohorts after 1985 involved populations in which some percentage had received treatment, prophylaxis, and/or antiretroviral treatment.

Within industrialized countries (and elite hospital settings of the Third World), the era of untreated HIV/AIDS patients is long past. Essentially, current modelers and clinicians in industrial countries retain no memory of HIV's natural disease course (natural history) in untreated patient cohorts.

5.3. Antenatal HIV Sero-Survey Findings

Annually, the RSA conducts a sero-prevalence of approximately 400 antenatal clinics. In the last 4 years, approximately 30,000 women have participated each year. The survey tests first-time pregnant mothers for the HIV antibody. In these sero-surveys, the percentage of pregnant women who were HIV-positive increased from 1% in 1990 to 30% in 2004.[16, 215, 216]

The RSA uses the findings of the national sero-survey to calculate an estimated overall HIV prevalence for the entire country, using modeling methods analogous to those applied by WHO and UNAIDS.[16, 90] Per Statistics South Africa: "Our knowledge of the HIV epidemic in

South Africa is based primarily on the prevalence data collected annually from pregnant women attending public antenatal clinics (ANC) since 1990."[90]

Granting such validity to sero-survey outcomes is seemingly inappropriate, particularly in the light of RSA death notifications findings. It is generally understood that medical assays are likely to generate more false-positives than true-positives in a large healthy asymptomatic population. [217, 218] Therefore, in the United States, very few assays are approved for screening large populations of asymptomatic people. Overall, assays are most accurate in a diseased population. Assays are best applied in a clinical setting in which patients are pre-screened by their medical history or clinical symptoms, the assay outcomes are only one component of the diagnostic algorithm, and patient follow-up confirms the diagnosis and efficacy of treatment. Generally, diagnostic assays are intended to confirm or substantiate a disease condition indicated by prior clinical and/or laboratory work-up. Table 13 lists the seroprevalence rates among South African women screened at antenatal clinics from 1990 to 2009.

Regarding HIV assays in particular, the market needs are dominated by the blood testing services. As stated by WHO: "To serve the needs of blood transfusion services, which use the vast majority of all HIV tests worldwide, increasingly sensitive HIV antibody assays have been developed in order to shorten the window period (*the interval between the point of infection and the development of detectable antibody*).[*] As a result of this trend, less sensitive but highly specific HIV tests have been withdrawn from the market."[228] Within this context, the words "increasingly sensitive" mean that assays generate more false-positives under these circumstances.

_____

[*] definitive *phrase* in Italics added by Author

Table 13 – HIV Prevalence Women at Antenatal Clinics in the RSA

Year	Survey Period	No. of Samples	HIV Prevalence	ref
1990	—	—	0.7%	[219]
1991	—	—	1.7%	[219]
1992	—	—	2.1%	[219]
1993	—	—	4%	[219]
1994	—	—	7.6%	[219]
1995	—	—	10.4%	[219]
1996	—	—	14.2%	[219]
1997	—	—	17%	[219]
1998	May 1987 – Oct 1998	104 683	0.22%	[220]
1998	—	—	22.4%	[221]
1999	—	—	22.8%	[221]
2000	October 2000	16 548	24.5%	[221]
2001	October 2001	16 743	24.8%	[222]
2002	October 2002	—	26.5%	[223, 224]
2003	October 2003	16 643	27.9%	[215, 223]
2004	October 2004	16 061	29.5%	[215, 216]
2005	October 2005	16 510	30.2%	[216]
2006	October 2006	33,034	29.1%	[225]
2007	October 2007	33 488	28.0%	[226]
2008	October 2008	33 927	29.3%	[8]
2009	October 2009	32 861	29.4%	[227]

However, even given these allowances, the high percentages of HIV seroprevalence in the RSA (and some other African and tropical settings) seems inordinate. In truth, no satisfactory explanation yet exists for such high levels of presumed false-positive rates within some Third World settings. The current consensus is to grant these findings validity, and derive some other explanation for the discordant findings. Nevertheless, the most widely available epidemiological data on HIV/AIDS in Africa are seroprevalence data.[229, 230]

6. TUBERCULOSIS & OTHER KILLERS

To put the HIV/AIDS mortality rates in perspective, Table 14 compares the RSA mortality data of HIV/AIDS with those of *tuberculosis*, *influenza and pneumonia*, and *intestinal infectious diseases* between 1997 and 2008.

Tuberculosis, *influenza and pneumonia*, and *intestinal infectious diseases* consistently stand as the ten leading underlying causes of death. In 2007, these three diseases were the first, second, and third leading underlying causes of death, respectively. Tuberculosis mortality rates have climbed for 20 years, prompting one author in 2011 to call RSA's tuberculosis strategy a "failure."[231] All three disease codes had higher rates of growth than of HIV/AIDS between 1997 and 2008:

Disease	Rate of Growth
Tuberculosis	3.4
Influenza and pneumonia	4.0
Intestinal infectious diseases	6.0
Human immunodeficiency virus [HIV] diseases	2.4

The working hypothesis is that HIV/AIDS is under-reported because HIV disease is being misclassified as other diseases. An alternate hypothesis is that, due to the burgeoning epidemics of *tuberculosis*, *influenza and pneumonia*, and *intestinal infectious diseases*, people infected with these typical diseases are being misclassified as having HIV/AIDS – a hypothesis proposed by other authors[78-80, 232] – perhaps diminishing the 2.4 growth rate observed for HIV disease in the RSA.

In 1993, the CDC added tuberculosis as an AIDS-defining condition, setting the world standard. This addition has been criticized because tuberculosis can be contracted without having HIV infection and/or impairment of cellular immunity.[79, 80] (However, the clearance of tuberculosis requires a competent cell mediated immunity, which HIV disrupts; making tuberculosis resistant to cure. *Mycobacterium tuberculosis* is a fungus-like bacterium.)

Table 14 – Tuberculosis, Pneumonias, and Intestinal Infections

	1997	%	1998	%	1999	%	2000	%	2001	%	2002	%	2003	%	2004	%	2005	%	2006	%	2007	%	2008	%	Growth Factor
Tuberculosis	22,021	6.9	28,487	7.7	34,173	8.9	42,102	10.2	50,872	11.3	59,951	12.0	67,609	12.2	69,689	12.3	73,903	12.5	76,402	12.6	76,761	12.8	74,863	12.6	3.4
Influenza & pneumonia	11,503	3.6	17,019	4.6	19,135	5.0	24,580	5.9	31,495	7.0	37,637	7.5	45,351	8.2	45,376	8.0	45,596	7.7	52,791	8.7	49,722	8.3	45,602	7.7	4.0
Intestinal infectious diseases	6,522	2.0	8,780	2.4	11,155	2.9	14,139	3.4	16,060	3.6	19,836	4.0	24,394	4.4	26,581	4.7	28,548	4.8	39,239	6.5	37,398	6.2	39,351	6.6	6.0
HIV disease	6,234	2.0	7,266	2.0	9,925	2.6	10,420	2.5	9,212	2.0	10,425	2	11,650	2.1	13,319	2.3	14,532	2.5	14,783	2.4	13,521	2.2	15,097	2.5	2.4
Ref	11		11		11		11		11		11.1		2		2		12		13		7		9		

IDC-10 Codes:

Tuberculosis A15 - A19
Influenza and pneumonia J10 – J18
Intestinal infectious diseases A00 - A09
Human immunodeficiency virus [HIV] diseases B20 – B24

Growth Factor calculated by Author

7. DISCUSSION

Mortality and survival rates of the magnitude presented in Tables 9, 10, and 11 represent the mortality of HIV infection among US and Europeans AIDS patients in absence of effective prophylactic or anti-retroviral regimens. These patients died despite the best of world-class hospitals and life support measures available (for some segments of the U.S. and European AIDS populations).

These findings do not necessarily countermand the existence of individuals, or some portion of the HIV-infected population that survive for 11 years without treatment or experience a silent 10-year incubation period. However, these findings indicate that a substantial portion of any HIV/AIDS patient population will die within 12 months of manifesting opportunistic infection(s).

Investigations based on interviews with AIDS patients indicated that silent incubation in some subset of the AIDS population averaged 8 to 24 months. The numbers of patients represented in these investigations were small, but when the focus of scientific investigation was centered on this endeavor, these were the findings (transfusion recipients seem to have longer incubation periods). Excepting these initial reports, other incubation estimates are models. There is no large database of raw empirical data detailing incubation for hundreds or thousands of patients. Rather, the incubation periods imputed into the computer models are mathematical models themselves.[176, 194-201]

Thus, in a cohort of untreated people living with HIV/AIDS (PLWH), some unspecified portion will begin manifesting opportunistic symptoms 8 to 24 months following infection, and roughly 50% of patients will die within 12 months of manifesting opportunistic infections, as indicated by the aforementioned tables. As seen in Table 12, evidence from 16,343 AIDS patients indicates that the 5-year survival rate, after manifesting opportunistic infections, was only 2% to 5% in untreated AIDS patients.[*]

Perhaps some portion of the population may survive 11 years — or persist 10 years symptom-free — but this proportion of the population may not be the majority. In current conceptions of patient survival, the majority of deaths should be clustered closely around the mean. This concept does not seem appropriate, given the well-documented natural course of HIV infection. Rather, the data points of the curve will be distributed over a 9-year period (from 2 years to 11 years post-infection), but the shape of the distribution curve remains undefined, due to the lack of any sufficient database of empirical evidence. In the modeled incubation estimates, the shapes of the curves projecting 10-year incubation periods have been filtered through pre-selected distribution curves using mixtures of raw and imputed data.[176, 194-201]

The Republic of South Africa (RSA) stands as the principal exemplar of the discrepancy between modeled HIV/AIDS estimates, surveillance data, and death counts. Yet, given the empirical death notification outcomes, Statistics South Africa, the RSA Department of Health, and other interested parties do not grant validity to these death tabulations. Rather, they hypothesize a series of misclassifications to explain away the missing numbers, despite the scale of the discrepancy.[91, 92, 94] The unquantifiable specter of social censure is also another presumed contributor to these consecutive misclassifications.[**]

The situation may best be described in the words of Stephen Jay Gould: "Facts do not 'speak for themselves', they are read in the light of theory."[233] The operative working hypothesis is that HIV/AIDS is pandemic in the Republic of South Africa and under-reported because HIV disease is being misclassified as other diseases due to inadequate surveillance systems.

An alternate hypothesis is that, due to the burgeoning epidemics of *tuberculosis, influenza and pneumonia*, and *intestinal infectious diseases* manifesting in the RSA, people infected with these typical diseases are being misclassified as having HIV/AIDS – again, a

---

[*] The number 16,343 (4,323 + 12,020) represents two of the studies cited in Table 12.
[**] Personal communication with Statistics South Africa

hypothesis proposed by other authors.[78-80, 232]

Furthermore, as viewed through the lens of Statistics South Africa, the RSA has an "African-type" epidemic.[24] In fact, per the reporting methods of Statistics South Africa, African Blacks are the only population group that has HIV/AIDS in the RSA. Per Statistics South Africa, HIV/AIDS is absent in the other RSA population groups (See Appendix F: *The HIV Club – Blacks Only.*)

"African-type" AIDS epidemics have been reported in the RSA, numerous other African countries including the Republic of the Congo (formerly known as Zaire), and Haiti. In "African-type" epidemics:

- the primary mode of HIV transmission is heterosexual;

- the number of HIV-infected women equals or exceeds the number of HIV-infected men;

- HIV/AIDS is said to be the primary harbinger of death; and

- the efficacy of heterosexual HIV transmission exceeds all plausibility.

In populations afflicted with "African-type" AIDS epidemics, the native death rates are extraordinarily high compared with those of the developed world. For example, life expectancy at birth in the RSA is 53.3 years for males and 55.2 years for females.[90] In the Republic of the Congo (formerly known as Zaire), which is consistently and mistakenly reported as the epicenter of the global AIDS epidemic, life expectancy is 55 years. In Haiti, also once fleetingly thought to be the epicenter of the AIDS epidemic, life expectancy at birth is 30 years.[234, 235]

All these populations are afflicted by communicable diseases, e.g., tuberculosis, other pneumonias, and intestinal infections, as well as the other miscellaneous adverse health conditions secondary to poverty, such as malnutrition and likely exposure to insanitary water. Per Statistics South Africa, HIV disease as a cause of death peaks around 30-39 years of age, then declines at older ages; the same age pattern seen with *all infectious diseases*, including *tuberculosis* and *malaria*, as well as *nutritional deficiencies*.[16]

Collectively, these populations also exhibit high HIV seropositivity rates. Thus, although *all infectious diseases*, *tuberculosis*, *malaria*, and *nutritional deficiencies* themselves might not cause false-positives on the HIV assays, these conditions might be markers for populations that render high false-positive rates, although the causative factor(s) remain uncharacterized. Effectively, members of these populations seem to have immunological systems chronically inflamed in a manner that prompts reactivity with the antigens (HIV viral proteins) and/or substrate of the HIV assays.

In Africa, seroprevalence data are the most widely available epidemiological data on HIV/AIDS.[229, 230] "In the majority of countries, the HIV epidemic has been monitored through [seroprevalence of] sentinel populations of women attending antenatal clinics, and vulnerable populations such as patients with sexually transmitted infections, intravenous drug users, men who have sex with men, or sex workers."[109]

Altogether, the situation represents an opportunity for improved assays and/or the repositioning of assays within improved clinical diagnostic algorithms specific to these populations (i.e., designing new diagnostic algorithms). The fault here is not with the tools, but with their application, and the validity granted to their current findings. These faults are consequent to the operative working theory, not the tools themselves.

This path of reasoning also allows one to examine some of the startling non-sequiturs of the "African-like" AIDS epidemics. For example, as stated in *AIDS Epidemic Update December 2005* (UNAIDS/WHO): "In many countries, marriage, and women's own fidelity are not enough to protect them against HIV infection. Among women surveyed in Harare (Zimbabwe), Durban and Soweto (South Africa), 66% reported having one lifetime partner, 79% had abstained from sex at least until the age of 17 (roughly the average age of first sexual encounter in most countries in the world). Yet, 40% of the young women were HIV-positive."[236]

These statements are non-sequiturs. Objectively – taken in sequence – they make no sense. Viewed in light of the current working hypothesis, this information prompts one to have tremendous empathy for these faultless women. However, viewed objectively, such rates of heterosexual transmission are entirely implausible: beyond the limits of physical reality in terms of heterosexual HIV transmission.

For example, the estimated risk of HIV transmission during male-to-male anal receptive intercourse is 0.005–0.02 per exposure (for the receptive partner). The estimated risk of HIV transmission during male-to-female vaginal intercourse is 0.001 per exposure (for the receptive partner).[237, 238] * Therefore, the theoretical risk rate of HIV transmission during unprotected anal intercourse is 5 to 20 times greater than that of unprotected vaginal intercourse.

To translate these risks into human terms, an examination of homosexual male sexual activity is in order. In a 1983 poll of White gay men in Johannesburg, 48% reported having over 20 sex partners in the preceding 12-month period ($n = 250$).[24] Prior to the advent of AIDS, gay males in the New York City region had twice the sexual proclivity of their RSA counterparts. Gay males in the NYC region were surveyed as averaging 19 – 20 sex partners in a 6-month period ($n = 674$; $n = 1,083$),[103, 239] or approximately 1000 sexual partners in a life-time.[104]

In the aforementioned study in which the CDC determined a median 7.5 month incubation period in 6 AIDS patients (among a population of 40 sexual contacts),[124] one patient reported an estimated 250 different male sexual partners each year from 1979 through 1981 and was able to name 72 of his 750 partners for this three-year period. (Reminder: not all gay males are highly sexually active.)

At the beginning of the AIDS epidemic, AIDS underwent geometric growth. From 1979 to 1982, the number of AIDS cases doubled every 6 months.[22] By 1985, the number of AIDS cases had slowed to a doubling every 12 months.[131, 132] The greater majority of the initial

---

* By a third account, the per exposure risk rate is 0.005–0.032 for anal intercourse and 0.0001 to 0.003 for vaginal intercourse. The numbers discussed above represent the most conservative comparison of transmission rates, i.e., the highest estimated rates of transmission.

AIDS patients had engaged in high-risk sexual behavior, i.e., anal intercourse. Again, the estimated rate of HIV transmission during receptive anal intercourse is 5 – 20 times greater than during receptive vaginal intercourse.

Therefore, theoretically, the heterosexual African Black men of the RSA would have to sleep with 5 – 20 as many sex partners as the gay men of NYC in order to instigate a geometrical AIDS growth pattern equaling that in the United States at the start of the AIDS epidemic. To provide the same level of opportunity for the sexual transmission of HIV as seen in the early American AIDS epidemic, the African Black heterosexual men would require sexual contact with approximately 100 – 400 partners every six months.

For their part, females also would not be allowed to be passive. The estimate risk of HIV transmission from female-to-male during unprotected vaginal intercourse is 0.0003 – 0.0009 per exposure. [237, 238, 240] These figures indicate that male-to-female HIV transmission is 1.1 to 3.3 times as effective as female-to-male HIV transmission during unprotected vaginal intercourse. Given the relative per exposure transmission rates, African Black heterosexual females would require approximately 1.1 to 3.3 times as many sexual partners as African Black heterosexual males to provide the same statistical opportunity for comparable HIV transmission.

Thus, in places such as Durban and Soweto, South Africa (mentioned above), the reportedly few sexually active women (and/or female prostitutes) would have to keep exceptionally busy to infect a roughly equal number of HIV-infected men (the sex ratio of HIV/AIDS patients in the RSA is roughly 1-to-1 with the females sometimes having slight predominance). By Department of Health estimates, 17.3% of adults 15 – 49 years of age in the Republic of South Africa were infected with HIV in 2010.[90] Comparatively, per CDC estimate, 0.6% of adults in the United States over 15 years of age are infected with HIV.[241]

No doubt, the general conception is that African societies, given their history of polygamy, must have high levels of sexual activity and partner exchange. However, in most regions of the world, "monogamy is the dominant pattern in most regions; but reporting of multiple partnerships is more common in men than women, and generally more common in developed countries than in developing countries . . . . Sexual activity in young single people tends to be sporadic, but is greater in industrialized countries than in developing countries."[242]

(These rudimentary calculations presented above should not be considered quantitatively accurate. Rather, these numbers should be used qualitatively, i.e., 'Given these theoretical transmission rates, and the different social climes of gay men in New York City and the rural villages of South Africa — does the concept of a decimating heterosexual HIV/AIDS epidemic among the rural populations of South Africa seem possible?' The qualitative question is: Does this concept of an exclusively Black heterosexual HIV/AIDS epidemic 'Pass' or 'Fail' ?)

Overall, the problem is that, as viewed through the lens of the operative working theory, facts and perceptions such as these pass unnoticed, or are not granted their appropriate juxtaposition within the conceptual framework.

In consideration of the existing conceptual framework, both Statistics South Africa and the RSA Department of Health grant greater validity to the operative working theory than to the empirical data at hand. The authorities believe that a gross number of HIV/AIDS deaths exist beyond the scope of their surveillance systems.

Given the prevailing conceptual, bureaucratic, and professional winds, would not clinicians have a tendency to overwrite rather than underwrite HIV disease as a cause of death, despite prevailing societal norms? (How stigmatizing can HIV/AIDS be, if HIV/AIDS accounts for 48% of deaths?) Given this existence of such a possible bias, the findings of the aforementioned RSA interim report seem questionable.

To repeat, Statistic South Africa compiled an interim report of all deaths in 1997 – 2001 utilizing a 12% sample. During the compilation of this interim report, disease codes were assigned by health professionals who interpreted the *causes of death* listed on the death notification forms, i.e., by hand.[93] During this subjective process, sitting in an office reviewing

death notification forms, and given the prevailing conceptual, bureaucratic, and professional

winds, would such health professionals likely misclassify actual cases of *all infectious diseases*;

certain disorders of the immune mechanism; *tuberculosis*; *malaria, nutritional deficiencies, non-*

communicable respiratory diseases, all sexually transmitted diseases, bacterial meningitis,

protein energy malnutrition; and certain *maternal conditions* as HIV/AIDS?

Yet the concepts utilized by Statistics South African and the RSA Department of Health

did not develop in a vacuum: they are in accordance with worldwide scientific and medical

consensus. Unfortunately, this consensus is subject to several severe distortions created by the

undue amplification of a select data subset by the general and scientific media. Although much

of this unduly amplified subset is valid, its selective presentation has rendered an operative

theory that lacks empirical substantiation.

Moreover, several key elements of the operative theory are based on erroneous

conclusions and/or concepts, which have become accepted hearsay within the public and

scientific domains. (The concept of the median 10-year incubation/survival period being one

such example. A second example is the theory that HIV originated in African primates. But this

theory was, in fact, instigated by an incident of laboratory contamination. The contamination

error was noted and corrected in a major scientific journal; but the correction passed unnoticed

by the scientific community at large.)[*]

Unfortunately, a series of interlocking fallacies have distorted scientific and public

perceptions of HIV and the AIDS epidemic. In this distortion, the basic theorem for the origin-

of-AIDS-in-Africa hypothesis is that HIV was endemic in Africa for 30 or 40 years before

ecological and sociological changes forced it out of the jungle. Once exposed to naïve, urban,

highly susceptible populations, the disease spread exponentially, eventually infecting tens or

---

[*] beyond the scope of this document, but described and referenced in *HIV/AIDS – The Facts and the Fiction*, Health
Alert Communications

hundreds of millions of Africans (without anybody noticing) before reaching across the Atlantic to selectively infect gay men in New York City. These fallacies form the foundation of scientific belief. As such, they have created a belief structure in which scientific and medical data are viewed through a warped lens.

The explanation of the reasoning behind these statements is beyond the scope of the document, but the data, reasoning, and references are provided in **HIV/AIDS - The Facts and The Fiction**, to which this book is adjuvant. This book, **HIV/AIDS in South Africa - The Facts and The Fiction**, provides numerical substantiation to some of the explanatory assertions presented in **HIV/AIDS - The Facts and The Fiction**.

HIV/AIDS - The Facts and The Fiction describes how these misconceptions developed during the tumultuous advent of AIDS into the human domain. Reporting on all the relevant disciplines, the book presents information previously overlooked, and reconfigures the AIDS scenario into a new, workable conceptual constellation; redefining the size, scale, and scope of the HIV/AIDS epidemic as depicted by data of the scientific and medical literature. In doing so, it expands upon many themes touched upon in this book.

The Republic of South Africa stands as exemplar of the discrepancies between the estimates and other sources of surveillance data. This situation is undoubtedly replicated throughout numerous other Third World settings. **HIV/AIDS - The Facts and The Fiction** describes the fallacies and distortions that gave rise to the current unworkable theories of the HIV/AIDS epidemic.

8. SUMMARY

In service to the reader, the Author reluctantly summarizes this document by providing numerical estimates for the burden of HIV/AIDS in the Republic of South Africa (RSA). The Author lacks the financial resources and the expertise for epidemiological modeling. Therefore, the best approach is to extrapolate a series of rudimentary estimates by utilizing existing empirical data. Thus, this document provides three sets of extrapolations utilizing empirical data as filtered through three theoretical frameworks:

- an estimate(s) derived from death tabulations in the RSA;

- an estimate derived from applying similar rates as those exhibited by HIV/AIDS patients during the early years of the U.S. HIV/AIDS epidemic; and

- an estimate derived from applying a similar HIV prevalence rate as currently seen in the United States.

In the first two sets of extrapolations, the Author will utilize HIV/AIDS statistical data for 1997 because an examination of the past best allows us to understand the current situation.

According to the health and mortality surveillance mechanisms operative in the RSA, the HIV/AIDS epidemic in the RSA is almost exclusively a phenomenon of the heterosexual African Black population (a demographically defined group). Therefore, this demographic group – the heterosexual African Black population – is the primary focus of the following discussion.

8.1.   Estimates Derived from RSA Death Tabulations

For the year 1997, the RSA attributed 6,235 deaths to HIV/AIDS. The RSA estimates that the 2,887,654 death notification forms processed for 1997 represented 81% of actual total deaths. Given that 6,235 represents an estimated 81% of all HIV deaths, and allowing an equal expansion across all *causes of death*, then 7,697 represents the "actual" number of HIV deaths in 1997, as attributed by tabulation of death notifications. If these figures were granted validity, then the number of HIV/AIDS deaths in 1997 ranged from approximately 6,235 to 7,697.

However, UNAIDS estimated that the RSA had 140,000 HIV/AIDS deaths in 1997. The health authorities in the RSA grant validity to the UNAIDS estimates; therefore, they utilize computer models that provide results approaching concordance with the UNAIDS estimates; believing that a vast number of HIV/AIDS cases either pass unreported and/or are miscoded (i.e., recorded under other *causes of death*) during the death tabulation process.

A research group respected by the RSA health authorities, *Groenewald et al.*, estimated that 48% of all deaths in the RSA between 1996 and 2006 were HIV/AIDS deaths. The RSA recorded a total of 317,132 deaths for 1997. Given that 317,132 represents an estimated 81% of all deaths in the RSA, then the estimated number of total deaths for the year 1997 was 391,520. Allowing 48% of these deaths to be attributed to HIV/AIDS deaths, then the estimated number of HIV/AIDS deaths in 1997 was 187,929.

Given this combination of empirical data and estimates, the number of presumed HIV/AIDS deaths in 1997 ranged from approximately 6,000 to 190,000. In the Author's opinion, the empirical value of 6,000 should be granted far greater validity in any discussion regarding the HIV/AIDS burden of the RSA; i.e., 6,000 should be the starting point of any discussion. Such discussion should consider whether 6,000 would be an overestimate. Is it possible that "HIV disease" is over-reported rather than under-reported on RSA death notification forms? Such over-reporting might arise from misdiagnoses of other diseases as HIV/AIDS due to: (1) the demonstrable inaccuracy of the HIV assays as diagnostic tools within indigent, tropical populations, and (2) the prevailing conceptual, bureaucratic, and professional "winds" that might prompt clinicians to interpret various common clinical symptoms as HIV/AIDS, particularly given false-positive findings from the HIV assays.

Also, the estimate of 190,000 HIV/AIDS deaths represents the theoretical number of HIV/AIDS deaths consequent to an "African-type" HIV/AIDS epidemic. In "African-type"

HIV/AIDS epidemics: (1) heterosexual HIV transmission is the dominant transmission vector; (2) the number of HIV-infected women equals or exceeds the number of HIV-infected men; (3) HIV/AIDS is said to be the primary harbinger of death; and (4) the efficacy of heterosexual HIV transmission exceeds all physical plausibility (the African Black heterosexual men would require sexual contact with approximately 100 – 400 partners every six months; and the heterosexual Black females would require 1.1 to 3.3 times as many sex partners as the heterosexual Black males to achieve the 1:1 male-to-female ratio of HIV/AIDS purported to exist in the RSA).

The heterosexual African Black population of the RSA is geographically and socially far removed from the epicenter of the HIV/AIDS epidemic (New York City). The Republic of South Africa also lacked the concentrated population of highly sexually active homosexual males (with open homosexual lifestyles) found only in the United States. Particularly at the beginning of the AIDS epidemic, this NYC gay lifestyle, enabling multiple sexual contacts several times a week, was fueled by a high level of disposable income among the homosexual male population of NYC. This, moreover, was coupled with an underlying economic apparatus dedicated to enabling this lifestyle, namely bath houses, bars, discos, and publications servicing this population.

The RSA also lacks the large black market in opiate and injectable drugs found in the United States and the Western world. (The logistics of opiate smuggling entail transfer of goods from third world economies to first world economies, providing the necessary extraordinary income source vital to high-risk smuggling). Thus, the RSA lacks both of the concentrated populations susceptible to the two primary modes of HIV transmission. Perhaps the Author is wrong in these suppositions, but the very concept of the "African-type" HIV/AIDS epidemic is based on the premise of heterosexual HIV transmission as the primary transmission vector.

8.2. Estimates Derived from U.S. Mortality Rates

Essentially, prior to 1985, AIDS patients in the United States lacked effective therapeutic and/or prophylactic drug regimens versus HIV infection and/or its consequent opportunistic infections. A similar situation exists for the millions of indigent African Blacks in the RSA purported to have HIV infection; therefore, we should see comparable patient outcomes, particularly given the ubiquitous nature of *Pneumocystis carinii*, which alone was responsible for roughly 50% of AIDS-related mortality in the United States prior to the availability of effective prophylaxis. Thus, the mortality rates among HIV/AIDS patients in the United States, during the early years of the epidemic, provide a theoretical framework for evaluating the HIV/AIDS burden of the RSA.

In the United States, between 1981 and 1983 (the first two years of the epidemic), 38% of patients diagnosed with AIDS had died. AIDS at that time was defined as having manifested opportunistic infections, most commonly *Pneumocystis carinii* pneumonia and Kaposi's sarcoma (KS). Allowing for a comparable mortality rate among the untreated, indigent, African Black heterosexual population, the deaths during these 2 years should account for approximately 38% of the living and dead AIDS patients in the RSA.

The combined, tabulated death count for 1997 and 1998 was 13,504. Given that 13,504 represented 38% of all existing AIDS patients in the RSA in 1997 (per the above definition), then the number of AIDS patients in the RSA in 1997 was approximately 35,536 AIDS patients, living and dead. This number represents only the theoretical number of patients with AIDS (as defined above), and does not address the unknown number of people with asymptomatic HIV infection. If the aforementioned combined death count for 1997 and 1998 accounted for only 81% of HIV/AIDS cases ($n = 13,504$), then the final figure would be a total of 43,871 living and dead AIDS patients in 1997.

By comparison, UNAIDS estimated that the RSA had 2.9 million people living with

HIV/AIDS (PLWH) in 1997. Even allowing an 11-year survival period, as inducted into the computer models, a substantial cluster of these people should have died by 2008. Yet, the RSA tabulated a total of 136,000 HIV/AIDS deaths for 1997 – 2008, inclusive.

The mortality rate of 38% was the lowest reported for a large cohort of AIDS patients (n = 1,972) in the United States. In all reports thereafter, the mortality rate among AIDS cases was typically 51% (or higher in later years).

[A further qualification of this data set: As reported in October 1996, the cumulative total of AIDS cases in the RSA was 12,825 cases (living and dead). This number represented all AIDS cases reported in the RSA between June 1981 and October 1996. (June 1981 is generally recognized as the beginning of the AIDS epidemic in the United States.)]

In 1997, the RSA had 140,000 HIV/AIDS deaths, achieving a cumulative total of HIV/AIDS deaths, that is, per UNAIDS estimate. The UNAIDS estimate for 1997 PLWH population in the RSA was 2.9 million. (These estimates were published in June 1998[1] – 18 months or so after the RSA had reported only 12,825 cumulative cases.]

8.3. Estimates Derived from an Assumed HIV Prevalence

By recent reports, the adult HIV prevalence in the United States is 0.6% and that of the Republic of South Africa is 17.3% among adults 15 – 49 years of age. This exceptionally high rate in the RSA was derived from computer models imputing: (1) an 8 – 11 year HIV incubation period, (2) a median survival of 11 years post-infection, and (3) sero-survey data derived from HIV assay testing among first-time pregnant women; giving rise to seropositivity rates of up to 30%. As described previously, computer outcomes utilizing these methodologies are highly questionable.

Actually, it is likely that the actual HIV prevalence in the RSA is less than that of the United States, due to: (1) the lack of concentrated populations susceptible to HIV transmission via unprotected anal intercourse and sharing IV needles, the two primary and most efficient transmission vectors; (2) the geographical and social distance of the heterosexual African Black population from the initial HIV/AIDS epicenters located in the United States. However, if we use the prevalence of the U.S. as a reference point, and grant the RSA an equivalent HIV prevalence rate of 0.6%, then the number of people living with HIV in the RSA is approximately 299,947 people (given an internal population estimate of 49,991,300 for 2010). Conversely, UNAIDS estimated that RSA had 5.6 million people living with HIV/AIDS in 2009.

Table 15 summaries the rudimentary extrapolations derived by utilizing empirical data as filtered through the three theoretical frameworks described in Section 8.1, Section 8.2, and Section 8.3 above.

Table 15 – Rudimentary Extrapolations for the HIV/AIDS Burden in the RSA

Description of Extrapolation	Number
Estimates Derived from RSA Death Tabulations (1997)	
• Number of ***HIV/AIDS deaths*** tabulated from death notification forms	6,235 to 7,697
• Estimate for ***HIV/AIDS deaths*** allowing for miscoding and under-reporting (i.e., 48% of all deaths)	187,929
• Corresponding UNAIDS estimate for ***HIV/AIDS deaths***	140,000
Estimates Derived from U.S. Mortality Rates (1998)	
• Estimated ***total number of living and dead HIV/AIDS patients***, derived from application of U.S. mortality rates (minimally 38%) to the tabulations of death notifications	35,536 to 43,871
• Corresponding UNAIDS estimate for ***people living with HIV/AIDS***	2,900,000
Estimates Derived from an Assumed HIV Prevalence (2009-2010)	
• Estimate of ***people living with HIV*** (PLWH) by applying an HIV prevalence rate equivalent to that of the United States (0.6%)	299,947
• Corresponding UNAIDS estimate for ***people living with HIV/AIDS***	5,600,000

9. ERRATA & UPDATES

This work was a labor of love that taxed everyone involved beyond all reasonable bounds. Undoubtedly, it contains grammatical, factual, citational, and conceptual errors, so please notify us when you find them (www.healthalert.net/Contact.html).

Errata and updates will be posted updated periodically at: www.healthalert.net/TFTF _errata&updates.pdf.

10. REFERENCES

1. UNAIDS/WHO. *Report on the global HIV/AIDS epidemic – June 1998.* Geneva, Switzerland June 1998.
2. Mortality and causes of death in South Africa, 2003 and 2004 Findings from death notification. In: Africa SS, ed. Pretoria, South Africa: Statistics South Africa; 2006.
3. UNAIDS. *Report on the global HIV/AIDS epidemic June 2000.* Geneva 27, Switzerland: UNAIDS; June 2000. ISBN: 92-9173-000-9; UNAIDS/00.13E (English original, June 2000).
4. UNAIDS. *2008 Report on the global AIDS epidemic.* Geneva, Switzerland 2008.
5. UNAIDS. *Global report: UNAIDS report on the global AIDS epidemic 2010.* Geneva, Switzerland 2010.
6. UNAIDS. *Report on the global HIV/AIDS epidemic July 2002.* Geneva, Switzerland July 2002.
7. Mortality and causes of death in South Africa, 2007: Findings from death notification. In: Africa SS, ed. Pretoria, South Africa: Statistics South Africa, Pretoria 2009.
8. 2008 National Antenatal Sentinel HIV & Syphilis Prevalence Survey: South Africa Report. In: Department of Health SA, ed. Pretoria, South Africa; 2009.
9. Mortality and causes of death in South Africa, 2008: Findings from death notification. In: Africa SS, ed. Pretoria, South Africa: Statistics South Africa, Pretoria; 2010.
10. UNAIDS/WHO. *AIDS epidemic update: December 2007.* Geneva, Switzerland December 2007. UNAIDS/07.27E / JC1322E.
11. Mortality and causes of death in South Africa, 1997-2003: Findings from death notifications. In: Africa SS, ed. Pretoria, South Africa: Statistics South Africa; 2005.
12. Mortality and causes of death in South Africa, 2005: Findings from death notification. In: Africa SS, ed. Pretoria, South Africa: Statistics South Africa, Pretoria; 2007.
13. Mortality and causes of death in South Africa, 2006: Findings from death notification. In: Africa SS, ed. Pretoria, South Africa: Statistics South Africa, Pretoria 2008.
14. CDC. Ten leading nationally notifiable infectious diseases--United States, 1995. *MMWR Morb Mortal Wkly Rep.* Oct 18 1996;45(41):883-884.
15. Disease Notification System. http://www.doh.gov.za/docs/dns-f.html. Accessed July 29, 2011.
16. Anderson B, Phillips H. Adult mortality (age 15-64) based on death notification data in South Africa: 1997-2004. In: Africa SS, ed. Pretoria, South Africa: Statistics South Africa; 2006.
17. WHO. Global AIDS surveillance. *Wkly Epidemiol Rec.* Jul 4 1997;72(27):197-198.
18. CDC. HIV/AIDS Surveillance Report. 1996;8(2).
19. CDC. Table II. Provisional cases of selected notifiable diseases, United States, weeks ending October 26, 1995, and October 28, 1996. *MMWR Morb Mortal Wkly Rep.* Nov 1 1996;45(43):954-955.
20. WHO. The HIV/AIDS situation, June 1998. *Wkly Epidemiol Rec.* June 26 1998;73(26):195-197.
21. CDC. Pneumocystis Pneumonia - Los Angeles. *MMWR Morb Mortal Wkly Rep.* June 5 1981;30(21):250-252.
22. CDC. Update on acquired immune deficiency syndrome (AIDS)--United States. *MMWR Morb Mortal Wkly Rep.* Sep 24 1982;31(37):507-508, 513-514.
23. Ras GJ, Simson IW, Anderson R, Prozesky OW, Hamersma T. Acquired immunodeficiency syndrome. A report of 2 South African cases. *S Afr Med J.* Jul 23 1983;64(4):140-142.

24. Sher R. HIV infection in South Africa, 1982-1988--a review. *S Afr Med J.* Oct 7 1989;76(7):314-318.

25. CDC. Acquired immunodeficiency syndrome (AIDS) update--United States. *MMWR Morb Mortal Wkly Rep.* Jun 24 1983;32(24):309-311.

26. CDC. Update: acquired immunodeficiency syndrome (AIDS)--United States. *MMWR Morb Mortal Wkly Rep.* Jun 22 1984;33(24):337-339.

27. CDC. Update: acquired immunodeficiency syndrome--United States. *MMWR Morb Mortal Wkly Rep.* May 10 1985;34(18):245-248.

28. Sher R. Acquired immune deficiency syndrome (AIDS) in the RSA. *S Afr Med J.* Oct 11 1986;Suppl:23-26.

29. CDC. Acquired Immunodeficiency Syndrome (AIDS) Weekly Surveillance Report - United States, December 29, 1986. https://www.cdc.gov/hiv/pdf/library/reports/surveillance/cdc-hiv-surveillance-report-1986.pdf.

30. WHO. Statistics from the World Health Organization and the Centers for Disease Control. *Aids.* Sep 1987;1(3):195-197.

31. WHO. Statistics from the World Health Organization and the Centers for Disease Control. *Aids.* Dec 1987;1(4):261-263.

32. WHO. Statistics from the World Health Organization and the Centers for Disease Control. *Aids.* April 1988;2(2):145-149.

33. WHO. Statistics from the World Health Organization and the Centers for Disease Control. *Aids.* Aug 1988;2(4):323-326.

34. WHO. Statistics from the World Health Organization and the Centers for Disease Control. *AIDS.* Jan 1989;3(1):51-54.

35. WHO. Statistics from the World Health Organization and the Centers for Disease Control. *AIDS.* Feb 1989;3(2):113-117.

36. WHO. Statistics from the World Health Organization and the Centers for Disease Control. *AIDS.* Mar 1989;3(3):187-190.

37. WHO. Statistics from the World Health Organization and the Centers for Disease Control. *AIDS.* May 1989;3(5):327-332.

38. WHO. Statistics from the World Health Organization and the Centers for Disease Control. *AIDS.* Jun 1989;3(6):405-409.

39. WHO. Statistics from the World Health Organization and the Centers for Disease Control. *AIDS.* Aug 1989;3(8):549-553.

40. WHO. Statistics from the World Health Organization and the Centers for Disease Control. *AIDS.* Sep 1989;3(9):619-623.

41. WHO. Statistics from the World Health Organization and the Centers for Disease Control. *AIDS.* Oct 1989;3(10):677-681.

42. WHO. Statistics from the World Health Organization and the Centers for Disease Control. *AIDS.* Nov 1989;3(11):771-775.

43. WHO. Statistics from the World Health Organization and the Centers for Disease Control. *AIDS.* Dec 1989;3(12):863-867.

44. WHO. Acquired immunodeficiency syndrome (AIDS)--data as at 31 December 1989. *Wkly Epidemiol Rec.* Jan 5 1990;65(1):1-2.

45. WHO. Acquired immunodeficiency syndrome (AIDS)--data as at 31 January 1990. *Wkly Epidemiol Rec.* Feb 2 1990;65(5):29-30.

46. WHO. Acquired immunodeficiency syndrome (AIDS)--data as at 30 April 1990. *Wkly Epidemiol Rec.* May 4 1990;65(18):133-134.

47. WHO. Acquired immunodeficiency syndrome (AIDS)--data as at 31 July 1990. *Wkly Epidemiol Rec.* Aug 3 1990;65(31):237-238.

48. WHO. Acquired immunodeficiency syndrome (AIDS)--data as at 31 August 1990. *Wkly Epidemiol Rec.* Sep 7 1990;65(36):273-274.

49. WHO. Acquired immunodeficiency syndrome (AIDS)--data as at 30 September 1990. *Wkly Epidemiol Rec.* Oct 5 1990;65(40):305-306.

50. WHO. Acquired immunodeficiency syndrome (AIDS)--data as at 31 October 1990. *Wkly Epidemiol Rec.* Nov 2 1990;65(44):337-338.

51. WHO. Acquired immunodeficiency syndrome (AIDS)--data as at 1 May 1991. *Wkly Epidemiol Rec.* May 3 1991;66(18):125-128.

52. WHO. Statistics from the World Health Organization and the Centers for Disease Control. *Aids.* Feb 1992;6(2):243-247.

53. WHO. Acquired immunodeficiency syndrome (AIDS)--data as at 31 December 1992. *Wkly Epidemiol Rec.* Jan 15 1993;68(3):9-10.

54. WHO. Acquired immunodeficiency syndrome (AIDS)--data as at 30 June 1993. *Wkly Epidemiol Rec.* Jul 2 1993;68(27):193-194.

55. WHO. Acquired immunodeficiency syndrome (AIDS)--data as at 31 December 1993. *Wkly Epidemiol Rec.* Jan 14 1994;69(2):5-6.

56. WHO. Acquired Immunodeficiency Syndrome (AIDS) - Data as at 30 June 1994. *Wkly Epidemiol Rec.* Jul 1 1994;69(26):189-190.

57. WHO. The current global situation of the HIV/AIDS pandemic. *Wkly Epidemiol Rec.* Jan 13 1995;70(2):7-8.

58. WHO. Acquired immunodeficiency syndrome (AIDS)--Data as at 30 June 1995. *Wkly Epidemiol Rec.* Jul 7 1995;70(27):193-194.

59. WHO. Acquired immunodeficiency syndrome (AIDS)--data as at 15 December 1995. *Wkly Epidemiol Rec.* Dec 15 1995;70(50):353-354.

60. WHO. Acquired immunodeficiency syndrome (AIDS)-data as at 30 June 1996. *Wkly Epidemiol Rec.* Jul 5 1996;71(27):205-206.

61. WHO. Acquired Immunodeficiency Syndrome (AIDS) - Data as at 20 November 1996. *Wkly Epidemiol Rec.* Nov 29 1996;71(48):361-362.

62. WHO. Global AIDS surveillance--part I. *Wkly Epidemiol Rec.* Nov 28 1997;72(48):357-358.

63. WHO. Global AIDS surveillance. *Wkly Epidemiol Rec.* Jun 26 1998;73(26):193-197.

64. WHO. Global AIDS surveillance--Part I. *Wkly Epidemiol Rec.* Nov 27 1998;73(48):373-376.

65. WHO. Global AIDS surveillance--Part I. *Wkly Epidemiol Rec.* Nov 26 1999;74(47):401-404.

66. WHO. Global AIDS surveillance. Part I. *Wkly Epidemiol Rec.* Nov 24 2000;75(47):379-383.

67. WHO. Global situation of the HIV/AIDS pandemic, end 2001. Part I. *Wkly Epidemiol Rec.* Dec 7 2001;76(49):381-386.

68. CDC. Table 16. AIDS cases, by persons' age category, exposure category, and sex, reported through December 2002—United States. December 2002; http://www.cdc.gov/hiv/surveillance/resources/reports/2002report/pdf/table16.pdf.

69. WHO. Global AIDS surveillance. Part II. *Wkly Epidemiol Rec.* Dec 14 2001;76(50):390-396.

70. WHO. The current global situation of the HIV/AIDS pandemic. *Wkly Epidemiol Rec.* Jan 15 1993;68(3):11.

71. UN. *Population in 1990 and 2000: All Countries*: Population Division, Department of Economic and Social Affairs, United Nations.

72. CDC. Update on Kaposi's sarcoma and opportunistic infections in previously healthy persons--United States. *MMWR Morb Mortal Wkly Rep.* Jun 11 1982;31(22):294, 300-291.

73. WHO. Statistics from the World Health Organization and the Centers for Disease Control. *Aids.* Feb 1988;2(1):65-69.

74. WHO. Statistics from the World Health Organization and the Centers for Disease Control. *Aids.* Jun 1988;2(3):235-238.

75. WHO. Global situation of the AIDS pandemic, end 2002. Part I. *Wkly Epidemiol Rec.* Dec 6 2002;77(49):417-424.

76. WHO. Acquired Immunodeficiency Syndrome (AIDS): WHO/CDC case definition for AIDS. *Wkly Epidemiol Rec.* March 7 1986;61(10):69-73.

77. WHO. Workshop on AIDS in Central Africa. Paper presented at: Workshop on AIDS in Central Africa; October 22-25, 1985, 1985; Banqui, Central African Republic.

78. Derbyshire SW. WHO criticised for "inflating" AIDS figures. *AIDS Anal Afr.* Dec 1995;5(6):4-5.

79. Gilks CF. What use is a clinical case definition for AIDS in Africa? *BMJ.* Nov 9 1991;303(6811):1189-1190.

80. Badri M, Ehrlich R, Pulerwitz T, Wood R, Maartens G. Tuberculosis should not be considered an AIDS-defining illness in areas with a high tuberculosis prevalence. *Int J Tuberc Lung Dis.* Mar 2002;6(3):231-237.

81. WHO. The current global situation of the HIV/AIDS pandemic. *Wkly Epidemiol Rec.* Jul 2 1993;68(27):195-196.

82. WHO. The current global situation of the HIV/AIDS pandemic. *Wkly Epidemiol Rec.* Jan 14 1994;69(2):7-8.

83. WHO. The current global situation of the HIV/AIDS pandemic. *Wkly Epidemiol Rec.* Jul 1 1994;69(26):191-192.

84. WHO. Acquired immunodeficiency syndrome (AIDS)--data as at 31 December 1994. *Wkly Epidemiol Rec.* Jan 13 1995;70(2):5-6.

85. WHO. The current global situation of the HIV/AIDS pandemic. *Wkly Epidemiol Rec.* Jul 7 1995;70(27):195-196.

86. WHO. The current global situation of the HIV/AIDS pandemic. *Wkly Epidemiol Rec.* Jul 5 1996;71(27):207-208.

87. WHO. The current global situation of the HIV/AIDS pandemic. *Wkly Epidemiol Rec.* Nov 29 1996;71(48):363-364.

88. WHO. The current global situation of the HIV/AIDS pandemic. *Wkly Epidemiol Rec.* Nov 28 1997;72(48):359-360.

89. WHO. Global situation of the HIV/ AIDS epidemic, end 2004. *Wkly Epidemiol Rec.* Dec 10 2004;79(50):441-449.

90. Mid-year population estimates 2010. In: Africa SS, ed. Pretoria, South Africa; 2010.

91. Groenewald P, Nannan N, Bourne D, Laubscher R, Bradshaw D. Identifying deaths from AIDS in South Africa. *AIDS.* Jan 28 2005;19(2):193-201.

92. Groenewald P, Bradshaw D, Dorrington R, Bourne D, Laubscher R, Nannan N. Identifying deaths from AIDS in South Africa: an update. *AIDS.* Apr 29 2005;19(7):744-745.

93. Causes of death in South Africa 1997-2001: Advance release of recorded causes of death. In: Africa SS, ed. Pretoria, South Africa; 2002.

94. Birnbaum JK, Murray CJ, Lozano R. Exposing misclassified HIV/AIDS deaths in South Africa. *Bull World Health Organ.* Apr 1 2011;89(4):278-285.

95. Edwards D, Harper PG, Pain AK, Welch J, Barbatis C, Mallinson C. Kaposi's sarcoma associated with AIDS in a woman from Uganda. *Lancet.* Mar 17 1984;1(8377):631-632.

96. Van de Perre P, Rouvroy D, Lepage P, et al. Acquired immunodeficiency syndrome in Rwanda. *Lancet.* Jul 14 1984;2(8394):62-65.

97. Piot P, Quinn TC, Taelman H, et al. Acquired immunodeficiency syndrome in a heterosexual population in Zaire. *Lancet.* Jul 14 1984;2(8394):65-69.

98. Clumeck N, Sonnet J, Taelman H, et al. Acquired immunodeficiency syndrome in African patients. *N Engl J Med.* Feb 23 1984;310(8):492-497.

99. Lyons SF, Schoub BD, McGillivray GM, Sher R, Dos Santos L. Lack of evidence of HTLV-III endemicity in southern Africa. *N Engl J Med.* May 9 1985;312(19):1257-1258.

100. Spracklen FH, Whittaker RG, Becker WB, Becker ML, Holmes CM, Potter PC. The acquired immune deficiency syndrome and related complex. A report of 2 confirmed cases in Cape Town with comments on human T-cell lymphotropic virus type III infections. *S Afr Med J.* Aug 3 1985;68(3):139-143.

101. CDC. Update: acquired immunodeficiency syndrome--United States. *MMWR Morb Mortal Wkly Rep.* Jan 17 1986;35(2):17-21.

102. Schoub BD, Lyons SF, McGillivray GM, Smith AN, Johnson S, Fisher EL. Absence of HIV infection in prostitutes and women attending sexually-transmitted disease clinics in South Africa. *Trans R Soc Trop Med Hyg.* 1987;81(5):874-875.

103. Szmuness W, Much I, Prince AM, et al. On the role of sexual behavior in the spread of hepatitis B infection. *Ann Intern Med.* Oct 1975;83(4):489-495.

104. Szmuness W, Dienstag JL, Purcell RH, Harley EJ, Stevens CE, Wong DC. Distribution of antibody to hepatitis a antigen in urban adult populations. *N Engl J Med.* Sep 30 1976;295(14):755-759.

105. Koblin BA, Morrison JM, Taylor PE, Stoneburner RL, Stevens CE. Mortality trends in a cohort of homosexual men in New York City, 1978-1988. *Am J Epidemiol.* Sep 15 1992;136(6):646-656.

106. Cohn RJ, MacPhail AP, Hartman E, Schwyzer R, Sher R. Transfusion-related human immunodeficiency virus in patients with haemophilia in Johannesburg. *S Afr Med J.* Dec 1 1990;78(11):653-656.

107. CDC. Table III. Cases of specified notifiable diseases, United States, weeks ending October 21, 1989 and October 22, 1989 (42nd Week). *MMWR Morb Mortal Wkly Rep.* Oct 27 1989;38(42):721-724.

108. CDC. HIV/AIDS Surveillance Centers for Disease Control; 1989.

109. UNAIDS. Improved methods and assumptions for estimation of the HIV/AIDS epidemic and its impact: Recommendations of the UNAIDS Reference Group on Estimates, Modelling and Projections. *AIDS.* Jun 14 2002;16(9):W1-14.

110. UNAIDS/UN. *The Demographic Impact of HIV/AIDS: Report on the Technical Meeting New York, 10 November 1998*: Population Division, Department of Economic and Social Affairs, United Nations Secretariat; February 1999 1999. ESA/P/WP.152* February 1999.

111. Brown T, Grassly NC, Garnett G, Stanecki K. Improving projections at the country level: the UNAIDS Estimation and Projection Package 2005. *Sex Transm Infect.* Jun 2006;82 Suppl 3:iii34-40.

112. Brown T, Bao L, Raftery AE, et al. Modelling HIV epidemics in the antiretroviral era: the UNAIDS Estimation and Projection package 2009. *Sex Transm Infect.* Dec 2010;86 Suppl 2:ii3-10.

113. Hogan DR, Zaslavsky AM, Hammitt JK, Salomon JA. Flexible epidemiological model for estimates and short-term projections in generalised HIV/AIDS epidemics. *Sex Transm Infect.* Dec 2010;86 Suppl 2:ii84-92.

114.   Salomon JA, Murray CJ. Modelling HIV/AIDS epidemics in sub-Saharan Africa using seroprevalence data from antenatal clinics. *Bull World Health Organ.* 2001;79(7):596-607.

115.   Cohen J. Epidemiology. New estimates scale back scope of HIV/AIDS epidemic. *Science.* Nov 30 2007;318(5855):1360-1361.

116.   CDC. The safety of hepatitis B virus vaccine. *MMWR Morb Mortal Wkly Rep.* Mar 18 1983;32(10):134-136.

117.   CDC. Current Trends Prevention of Acquired Immune Deficiency Syndrome (AIDS): Report of Inter-Agency Recommendations *MMWR Morb Mortal Wkly Rep.* March 04, 1983 1983;32(8):101-103.

118.   CDC. Unexplained immunodeficiency and opportunistic infections in infants--New York, New Jersey, California. *MMWR Morb Mortal Wkly Rep.* Dec 17 1982;31(49):665-667.

119.   Ammann AJ, Cowan MJ, Wara DW, et al. Acquired immunodeficiency in an infant: possible transmission by means of blood products. *Lancet.* Apr 30 1983;1(8331):956-958.

120.   Rubinstein A. Acquired immunodeficiency syndrome in infants. *Am J Dis Child.* Sep 1983;137(9):825-827.

121.   Shannon KM, Ammann AJ. Acquired immune deficiency syndrome in childhood. *J Pediatr.* Feb 1985;106(2):332-342.

122.   Anderson RM, Medley GF. Epidemiology of HIV infection and AIDS: incubation and infectious periods, survival and vertical transmission. *AIDS.* 1988;2 Suppl 1:S57-63.

123.   CDC. A cluster of Kaposi's sarcoma and Pneumocystis carinii pneumonia among homosexual male residents of Los Angeles and Orange Counties, California. *MMWR Morb Mortal Wkly Rep.* Jun 18 1982;31(23):305-307.

124.   Auerbach DM, Darrow WW, Jaffe HW, Curran JW. Cluster of cases of the acquired immune deficiency syndrome. Patients linked by sexual contact. *Am J Med.* Mar 1984;76(3):487-492.

125.   Gerstoft J, Nielsen JO, Dickmeiss E, Ronne T, Platz P, Mathiesen L. The acquired immunodeficiency syndrome (AIDS) in Denmark. A report from the Copenhagen study group of AIDS on the first 20 Danish patients. *Acta Med Scand.* 1985;217(2):213-224.

126.   Anderson KC, Gorgone BC, Marlink RG, et al. Transfusion-acquired human immunodeficiency virus infection among immunocompromised persons. *Ann Intern Med.* Oct 1986;105(4):519-527.

127.   Isaksson B, Albert J, Chiodi F, Furucrona A, Krook A, Putkonen P. AIDS two months after primary human immunodeficiency virus infection. *J Infect Dis.* Oct 1988;158(4):866-868.

128.   Vittecoq D, Autran B, Bourstyn E, Chermann JC. Lymphadenopathy syndrome and seroconversion two months after single use of needle shared with an AIDS patient. *Lancet.* May 31 1986;1(8492):1280.

129.   Fincher RM, de Silva M, Lobel S, Spencer M. AIDS-related complex in a heterosexual man seven weeks after a transfusion. *N Engl J Med.* Nov 7 1985;313(19):1226-1227.

130.   Pedersen C, Nielsen JO, Dickmeis E, Jordal R. Early progression to AIDS following primary HIV infection. *AIDS.* Jan 1989;3(1):45-47.

131.   Curran JW. The epidemiology and prevention of the acquired immunodeficiency syndrome. *Ann Intern Med.* Nov 1985;103(5):657-662.

132.   Jaffe HW, Hardy AM, Morgan WM, Darrow WW. The acquired immunodeficiency syndrome in gay men. *Ann Intern Med.* Nov 1985;103(5):662-664.

133.   CDC. HIV/AIDS Surveillance Report 1991. January 1992;8(2).

134. Paillaud E, Merlier I, Dupeyron C, Scherman E, Poupon J, Bories PN. Oral candidiasis and nutritional deficiencies in elderly hospitalised patients. *Br J Nutr.* Nov 2004;92(5):861-867.

135. Gracey M, Stone DE, Suharjono, Sunoto. Isolation of Candida species from the gastrointestinal tract in malnourished children. *Am J Clin Nutr.* Apr 1974;27(4):345-349.

136. Gross RL, Newberne PM. Role of nutrition in immunologic function. *Physiol Rev.* Jan 1980;60(1):188-302.

137. Parratt D. Nutrition and immunity. *Proc Nutr Soc.* May 1980;39(2):133-140.

138. Samaranayake LP. Nutritional factors and oral candidosis. *J Oral Pathol.* Feb 1986;15(2):61-65.

139. McMurray DN. Cell-mediated immunity in nutritional deficiency. *Prog Food Nutr Sci.* 1984;8(3-4):193-228.

140. Goldman AS, Goldman LR, Goldman DA. What caused the epidemic of Pneumocystis pneumonia in European premature infants in the mid-20th century? *Pediatrics.* Jun 2005;115(6):e725-736.

141. Hughes WT, Price RA, Sisko F, et al. Protein-calorie malnutrition. A host determinant for Pneumocystis carinii infection. *Am J Dis Child.* Jul 1974;128(1):44-52.

142. O'Brien TR, Kedes D, Ganem D, et al. Evidence for concurrent epidemics of human herpesvirus 8 and human immunodeficiency virus type 1 in US homosexual men: rates, risk factors, and relationship to Kaposi's sarcoma. *J Infect Dis.* Oct 1999;180(4):1010-1017.

143. Schulz TF. Kaposi's sarcoma-associated herpesvirus (human herpesvirus 8): epidemiology and pathogenesis. *J Antimicrob Chemother.* Apr 2000;45 Suppl T3:15-27.

144. Renwick N, Schulz T, Goudsmit J. *Kaposi's Sarcoma and Kaposi's Sarcoma-associated Herpesvirus/Human Herpesvirus 8: An Overview*: Los Alamos National Laboratory, Los Alamos, New Mexico; 1999.

145. O'Leary JJ, Kennedy MM, McGee JO. Kaposi's sarcoma associated herpes virus (KSHV/HHV 8): epidemiology, molecular biology and tissue distribution. *Mol Pathol.* Feb 1997;50(1):4-8.

146. Miles SA. Pathogenesis of human immunodeficiency virus-related Kaposi's sarcoma. *Curr Opin Oncol.* Oct 1992;4(5):875-882.

147. Chang Y, Ziegler J, Wabinga H, et al. Kaposi's sarcoma-associated herpesvirus and Kaposi's sarcoma in Africa. Uganda Kaposi's Sarcoma Study Group. *Arch Intern Med.* Jan 22 1996;156(2):202-204.

148. Nawar E, Mbulaiteye SM, Gallant JE, et al. Risk factors for Kaposi's sarcoma among HHV-8 seropositive homosexual men with AIDS. *Int J Cancer.* Jun 10 2005;115(2):296-300.

149. Mancuso R, Biffi R, Valli M, et al. HHV8 a subtype is associated with rapidly evolving classic Kaposi's sarcoma. *J Med Virol.* Dec 2008;80(12):2153-2160.

150. Matondo P. Kaposi's sarcoma and faecal-oral exposure. *Lancet.* Jun 13 1992;339(8807):1490.

151. Beral V, Bull D, Darby S, et al. Risk of Kaposi's sarcoma and sexual practices associated with faecal contact in homosexual or bisexual men with AIDS. *Lancet.* Mar 14 1992;339(8794):632-635.

152. Darrow WW, Peterman TA, Jaffe HW, Rogers MF, Curran JW, Beral V. Kaposi's sarcoma and exposure to faeces. *Lancet.* Mar 14 1992;339(8794):685.

153. Elford J, Tindall B, Sharkey T. Kaposi's sarcoma and insertive rimming. *Lancet.* Apr 11 1992;339(8798):938.

154. Page-Bodkin K, Tappero J, Samuel M, Winkelstein W. Kaposi's sarcoma and faecal-oral exposure. *Lancet.* Jun 13 1992;339(8807):1490.

155. O'Leary JJ. Seeking the cause of Kaposi's sarcoma. *Nat Med.* Aug 1996;2(8):862-863.

156. CDC. Revision of the case definition of acquired immunodeficiency syndrome for national reporting--United States. *MMWR Morb Mortal Wkly Rep.* Jun 28 1985;34(25):373-375.

157. CDC. Classification system for human T-lymphotropic virus type III/lymphadenopathy-associated virus infections. *MMWR Morb Mortal Wkly Rep.* May 23 1986;35(20):334-339.

158. CDC. 1993 revised classification system for HIV infection and expanded surveillance case definition for AIDS among adolescents and adults. *MMWR Recomm Rep.* Dec 18 1992;41(RR-17):1-19.

159. CDC. Follow-up on Kaposi's sarcoma and Pneumocystis pneumonia. *MMWR Morb Mortal Wkly Rep.* Aug 28 1981;30(33):409-410.

160. CDC. Kaposi's Sarcoma (KS), Pneumocystis Carinii Pneumonia (PCP), and Other Opportunistic Infections (OI): Cases Reported to CDC as sf July 8, 1982. *HIV Surveillance Report* [http://www.cdc.gov/hiv/topics/surveillance/resources/reports/pdf/surveillance82.pdf.

161. CDC. Acquired Immunodeficiency Syndrome (AIDS) Weekly Surveillance Report - United States, December 30, 1985. *HIV Surveillance Report* [http://www.cdc.gov/hiv/topics/surveillance/resources/reports/pdf/surveillance85.pdf.

162. CDC. Acquired Immunodeficiency Syndrome (AIDS) Weekly Surveillance Report - United States, December 31, 1984. *HIV Surveillance Report* [http://www.cdc.gov/hiv/topics/surveillance/resources/reports/pdf/surveillance84.pdf.

163. CDC. Acquired Immunodeficiency Syndrome (AIDS) Weekly Surveillance Report - United States, December 22, 1983. *HIV Surveillance Report* [http://www.cdc.gov/hiv/topics/surveillance/resources/reports/pdf/surveillance83.pdf.

164. CDC. Update: acquired immunodeficiency syndrome (AIDS)--United States. *MMWR Morb Mortal Wkly Rep.* Sep 9 1983;32(35):465-467.

165. CDC. Update: acquired immunodeficiency syndrome (AIDS) - United States. *MMWR Morb Mortal Wkly Rep.* Jan 6 1984;32(52):688-691.

166. Biggar RJ. AIDS incubation in 1891 HIV seroconverters from different exposure groups. International Registry of Seroconverters. *AIDS.* Nov 1990;4(11):1059-1066.

167. Gottlieb MS, Schroff R, Schanker HM, et al. Pneumocystis carinii pneumonia and mucosal candidiasis in previously healthy homosexual men: evidence of a new acquired cellular immunodeficiency. *N Engl J Med.* Dec 10 1981;305(24):1425-1431.

168. Gottlieb MS. Pneumocystis pneumonia--Los Angeles. *Am J Public Health.* Jun 1981;30:250-252.

169. Masur H, Michelis MA, Greene JB, et al. An outbreak of community-acquired Pneumocystis carinii pneumonia: initial manifestation of cellular immune dysfunction. *N Engl J Med.* Dec 10 1981;305(24):1431-1438.

170. Jaffe HW, Bregman DJ, Selik RM. Acquired immune deficiency syndrome in the United States: the first 1,000 cases. *J Infect Dis.* Aug 1983;148(2):339-345.

171. CDC. Epidemiologic aspects of the current outbreak of Kaposi's sarcoma and opportunistic infections. *N Engl J Med.* Jan 28 1982;306(4):248-252.

172. Johnson NM. Pneumonia in the acquired immune deficiency syndrome. *Br Med J (Clin Res Ed).* May 4 1985;290(6478):1299-1301.

173. Haverkos HW, Drotman DP. Prevalence of Kaposi's sarcoma among patients with AIDS. *N Engl J Med.* Jun 6 1985;312(23):1518.

174. Holmberg K, Meyer RD. Fungal infections in patients with AIDS and AIDS-related complex. *Scand J Infect Dis.* 1986;18(3):179-192.

175. Lemp GF, Payne SF, Neal D, Temelso T, Rutherford GW. Survival trends for patients with AIDS. *JAMA.* Jan 19 1990;263(3):402-406.

176. Jacobson LP, Kirby AJ, Polk S, et al. Changes in survival after acquired immunodeficiency syndrome (AIDS): 1984-1991. *Am J Epidemiol.* Dec 1 1993;138(11):952-964.

177. Harris JE. Improved short-term survival of AIDS patients initially diagnosed with Pneumocystis carinii pneumonia, 1984 through 1987. *JAMA.* Jan 19 1990;263(3):397-401.

178. CDC. Update: acquired immunodeficiency syndrome (AIDS)--United States. *MMWR Morb Mortal Wkly Rep.* Aug 5 1983;32(30):389-391.

179. United States AIDS activity. *Acquir Immunodefic Syndr (AIDS) Wkly Surveill Rep.* May 26 1986:1-3.

180. Moss AR, McCallum G, Volberding PA, Bacchetti P, Dritz S. Mortality associated with mode of presentation in the acquired immune deficiency syndrome. *J Natl Cancer Inst.* Dec 1984;73(6):1281-1284.

181. Stehr-Green JK, Holman RC, Mahoney MA. Survival analysis of hemophilia-associated AIDS cases in the US. *Am J Public Health.* Jul 1989;79(7):832-835.

182. CDC. Possible transfusion-associated acquired immune deficiency syndrome (AIDS) - California. *MMWR Morb Mortal Wkly Rep.* Dec 10 1982;31(48):652-654.

183. Hughes WT. Pneumocystis carinii pneumonia. *N Engl J Med.* Dec 22 1977;297(25):1381-1383.

184. Graham SM. Non-tuberculosis opportunistic infections and other lung diseases in HIV-infected infants and children. *Int J Tuberc Lung Dis.* Jun 2005;9(6):592-602.

185. Wakefield AE, Stewart TJ, Moxon ER, Marsh K, Hopkin JM. Infection with Pneumocystis carinii is prevalent in healthy Gambian children. *Trans R Soc Trop Med Hyg.* Nov-Dec 1990;84(6):800-802.

186. Hughes WT. Pneumocystis carinii pneumonitis. *Chest.* Jun 1984;85(6):810-813.

187. Pifer LL, Hughes WT, Stagno S, Woods D. Pneumocystis carinii infection: evidence for high prevalence in normal and immunosuppressed children. *Pediatrics.* Jan 1978;61(1):35-41.

188. Mahomed AG, Murray J, Klempman S, et al. Pneumocystis carinii pneumonia in HIV infected patients from South Africa. *East Afr Med J.* Feb 1999;76(2):80-84.

189. Fisk DT, Meshnick S, Kazanjian PH. Pneumocystis carinii pneumonia in patients in the developing world who have acquired immunodeficiency syndrome. *Clin Infect Dis.* Jan 1 2003;36(1):70-78.

190. Murray JF. Pulmonary complications of HIV-1 infection among adults living in Sub-Saharan Africa. *Int J Tuberc Lung Dis.* Aug 2005;9(8):826-835.

191. Madhi SA, Cutland C, Ismail K, O'Reilly C, Mancha A, Klugman KP. Ineffectiveness of trimethoprim-sulfamethoxazole prophylaxis and the importance of bacterial and viral coinfections in African children with Pneumocystis carinii pneumonia. *Clin Infect Dis.* Nov 1 2002;35(9):1120-1126.

192. CDC. Antibodies to a retrovirus etiologically associated with acquired immunodeficiency syndrome (AIDS) in populations with increased incidences of the syndrome. *MMWR Morb Mortal Wkly Rep.* Jul 13 1984;33(27):377-379.

193. CDC. Guidelines for effective school health education to prevent the spread of AIDS. *MMWR Morb Mortal Wkly Rep.* Jan 29 1988;37 Suppl 2:1-14.

194. Lui KJ, Lawrence DN, Morgan WM, Peterman TA, Haverkos HW, Bregman DJ. A model-based approach for estimating the mean incubation period of transfusion-associated acquired immunodeficiency syndrome. *Proc Natl Acad Sci U S A.* May 1986.

195. Lui KJ, Darrow WW, Rutherford GW, 3rd. A model-based estimate of the mean incubation period for AIDS in homosexual men. *Science.* Jun 3 1988;240(4857):1333-1335.

196. Muñoz A, Wang MC, Bass S, et al. Acquired immunodeficiency syndrome (AIDS)-free time after human immunodeficiency virus type 1 (HIV-1) seroconversion in homosexual men. Multicenter AIDS Cohort Study Group. *Am J Epidemiol.* Sep 1989;130(3):530-539.

197. Jaffe HW, Darrow WW, Echenberg DF, et al. The acquired immunodeficiency syndrome in a cohort of homosexual men. A six-year follow-up study. *Ann Intern Med.* Aug 1985;103(2):210-214.

198. Stevens CE, Taylor PE, Zang EA, et al. Human T-cell lymphotropic virus type III infection in a cohort of homosexual men in New York City. *JAMA.* Apr 25 1986;255(16):2167-2172.

199. Bacchetti P, Moss AR. Incubation period of AIDS in San Francisco. *Nature.* Mar 16 1989;338(6212):251-253.

200. Hessol NA, Koblin BA, van Griensven GJ, et al. Progression of human immunodeficiency virus type 1 (HIV-1) infection among homosexual men in hepatitis B vaccine trial cohorts in Amsterdam, New York City, and San Francisco, 1978-1991. *Am J Epidemiol.* Jun 1 1994;139(11):1077-1087.

201. Hessol NA, Lifson AR, O'Malley PM, Doll LS, Jaffe HW, Rutherford GW. Prevalence, incidence, and progression of human immunodeficiency virus infection in homosexual and bisexual men in hepatitis B vaccine trials, 1978-1988. *Am J Epidemiol.* Dec 1989;130(6):1167-1175.

202. Bacchetti P. Estimating the Incubation Period of AIDS by Comparing Population Infection and Diagnosis Patterns. *Journal of the American Statistical Association.* December 1990;85(412):1002-1008.

203. Burny A, Bruck C, Cleuter Y, et al. Bovine leukemia virus, a distinguished member of the human T-lymphotropic virus family. *Princess Takamatsu Symp.* 1984;15:219-227.

204. Oroszlan S, Copeland TD, Rice NR, et al. Structural and antigenic characterization of the proteins of human T-cell leukemia viruses and their relationships to the gene products of other retroviruses. *Princess Takamatsu Symp.* 1984;15:147-157.

205. Sonigo P, Alizon M, Staskus K, et al. Nucleotide sequence of the visna lentivirus: relationship to the AIDS virus. *Cell.* Aug 1985;42(1):369-382.

206. Stephens RM, Casey JW, Rice NR. Equine infectious anemia virus gag and pol genes: relatedness to visna and AIDS virus. *Science.* Feb 7 1986;231(4738):589-594.

207. Montagnier L, Dauguet C, Axler C, et al. A new type of retrovirus isolated from patients presenting with lymphadenopathy and acquired immune deficiency syndrome: Structural and antigenic relatedness with equine infectious anaemia virus. *Annales de l'Institut Pasteur. Virologie.* 1984;135(1):119-131, 133-134.

208. Goudsmit J, Houwers DJ, Smit L, Nauta IM. LAV/HTLV-III gag gene product p24 shares antigenic determinants with equine infectious anemia virus but not with visna virus or caprine arthritis encephalitis virus. *Intervirology.* 1986;26(3):169-173.

209. Gonda MA, Braun MJ, Carter SG, et al. Characterization and molecular cloning of a bovine lentivirus related to human immunodeficiency virus. *Nature.* Nov 26-Dec 2 1987;330(6146):388-391.

210. Gonda MA, Wong-Staal F, Gallo RC, Clements JE, Narayan O, Gilden RV. Sequence homology and morphologic similarity of HTLV-III and visna virus, a pathogenic lentivirus. *Science.* Jan 11 1985;227(4683):173-177.

211. Gonda MA, Braun MJ, Clements JE, et al. Human T-cell lymphotropic virus type III shares sequence homology with a family of pathogenic lentiviruses. *Proc Natl Acad Sci U S A.* Jun 1986;83(11):4007-4011.

212. Stover J. Projecting the demographic consequences of adult HIV prevalence trends: the Spectrum Projection Package. *Sex Transm Infect.* Aug 2004;80 Suppl 1:i14-18.

213. CDC. Estimates of HIV prevalence and projected AIDS cases: summary of a workshop, October 31-November 1, 1989. *MMWR Morb Mortal Wkly Rep.* Feb 23 1990;39(7):110-112, 117-119.

214. Zidovudine approved by FDA for treatment of AIDS. *Clin Pharm.* Jun 1987;6(6):431,435.

215. National HIV and Syphilis Antenatal Sero-Prevalence Survey in South Africa 2004. In: Department of Health SA, ed. Pretoria, South Africa; 2005.

216. National HIV and Syphilis Antenatal Sero-Prevalence Survey in South Africa 2005. In: Department of Health SA, ed. Pretoria, South Africa; 2006.

217. Proffitt MR, Yen-Lieberman B. Laboratory diagnosis of human immunodeficiency virus infection. *Infect Dis Clin North Am.* Jun 1993;7(2):203-219.

218. WHO. *Regional workshop on HIV testing strategies.* Amman, Jordan: World Health Organization Regional Office for the Eastern Mediterranean; June 26, 2006 2006.

219. WHO. HIV/AIDS surveillance and global estimates. Part II. *Wkly Epidemiol Rec.* Dec 13 2002;77(50):425-430.

220. Shapiro M, Crookes RL, O'Sullivan E. Screening antenatal blood samples for anti-human immunodeficiency virus antibodies by a large-pool enzyme-linked immunosorbent assay system. Results of an 18-month investigation. *S Afr Med J.* Sep 16 1989;76(6):245-247.

221. National HIV and Syphilis Sero-Prevalence Survey of women attending Public Antenatal Clinics in South Africa 2000. Pretoria, South Africa: Department of Health, South Africa; 2000.

222. National HIV and Syphilis Sero-Prevalence Survey In South Africa 2001. Pretoria, South Africa: Department of Health, South Africa; 2001.

223. Makubalo L, Netshidzivhani P, Mahlasela L, du Plessis R. *National HIV and Syphilis Antenatal Sero-Prevalence Survey in South Africa 2003* 2004.

224. National HIV and Syphilis Antenatal Sero-Prevalence Survey in South Africa 2002. In: Department of Health SA, ed. Pretoria, South Africa; 2002.

225. National HIV and Syphilis Antenatal Sero-Prevalence Survey in South Africa 2006. In: Department of Health SA, ed. Pretoria, South Africa; 2006.

226. The National HIV and Syphilis Prevalence Survey South Africa 2007. In: Department of Health SA, ed. Pretoria, South Africa; 2008.

227. National Antenatal Sentinel HIV and Syphilis Prevalence Survey in South Africa, 2009. In: Department of Health SA, ed. Pretoria, South Africa; 2010.

228. WHO. Joint United Nations Programme on HIV/AIDS (UNAIDS)-WHO. Revised recommendations for the selection and use of HIV antibody tests. *Wkly Epidemiol Rec.* Mar 21 1997;72(12):81-87.

229. Salomon J, Gakidou E, Murray J. *Methods for Modeling the HIV/AIDS Epidemic In Sub-Saharan Africa*: UNAIDS/WHO Working Group on Global HIV/AIDS and STD Surveillance.

230. Diaz T, De Cock K, Brown T, Ghys PD, Boerma JT. New strategies for HIV surveillance in resource-constrained settings: an overview. *AIDS.* May 2005;19 Suppl 2:S1-8.

231. Wood R, Lawn SD, Johnstone-Robertson S, Bekker LG. Tuberculosis control has failed in South Africa--time to reappraise strategy. *S Afr Med J.* Feb 2010;101(2):111-114.

232. Strecker W, Gurtler L, Schilling M, Binibangili M, Strecker K. Epidemiology and clinical manifestation of HIV infection in northern Zaire. *Eur J Epidemiol.* Feb 1994;10(1):95-98.

233. Gould S. *Ever Since Darwin*. New York: Norton; 1977.

234. CIA Factbook Haiti. https://www.cia.gov/library/publications/the-world-factbook/geos/ha.html. Accessed November 7, 2010.

235. CIA Factbook - Zaire (Democratic Republic of the Congo). https://www.cia.gov/library/publications/the-world-factbook/geos/cg.html. Accessed November 7, 2010.

236. UNAIDS/WHO. *AIDS Epidemic Update December 2005* December 2005.

237. Pinkerton SD, Martin JN, Roland ME, Katz MH, Coates TJ, Kahn JO. Cost-effectiveness of postexposure prophylaxis after sexual or injection-drug exposure to human immunodeficiency virus. *Arch Intern Med.* Jan 12 2004;164(1):46-54.

238. Smith DK, Grohskopf LA, Black RJ, et al. Antiretroviral postexposure prophylaxis after sexual, injection-drug use, or other nonoccupational exposure to HIV in the United States: recommendations from the U.S. Department of Health and Human Services. *MMWR Recomm Rep.* Jan 21 2005;54(RR-2):1-20.

239. Szmuness W, Stevens CE, Zang EA, Harley EJ, Kellner A. A controlled clinical trial of the efficacy of the hepatitis B vaccine (Heptavax B): a final report. *Hepatology.* Sep-Oct 1981;1(5):377-385.

240. Havens PL. Postexposure prophylaxis in children and adolescents for nonoccupational exposure to human immunodeficiency virus. *Pediatrics.* Jun 2003;111(6 Pt 1):1475-1489.

241. UN. Population and HIV/AIDS. In: population-hiv2010chart.pdf, ed. *PDF*. New York: Population Division, Department of Economic and Social Affairs; 2010.

242. Wellings K, Collumbien M, Slaymaker E, et al. Sexual behaviour in context: a global perspective. *Lancet.* Nov 11 2006;368(9548):1706-1728.

11. APPENDICES

11.1. Appendix A: Statistics South Africa vs. NCHS Ranking Methods

Table 15 compares outcomes between the two methods for the top ten leading underlying causes of death in 1999. For each death notification form, the underlying cause of death is derived automatically by a software program called Automated Classification of Medical Entities (ACME 2004.02) developed by the United States National Center for Health Statistics (NCHS) using ICD-10 coding (International Classification of Diseases, Version 10).[9, 11] Statistics South Africa modified the ICD codes to reflects the disease patterns, a common procedure.

Table 16 – Comparison of RSA and NCHS Ranking Methods, 1999

	Statistics South Africa	Number of deaths		NCHS ranking method (developed for use with ICD 10 according to recommendations by 1951 Public Health Conference)	Number of deaths
1	Events of undetermined intent (Y10 - Y34)	37 173	1	Diseases of heart	40 118
2	Tuberculosis (A15 - A19)	34 173	2	Tuberculosis	34 173
3	Other forms of heart disease (I30 - I52)	20 120	3	Malignant neoplasm	29 647
4	Cerebrovascular diseases (I60 - I69)	19 948	4	Certain conditions originating in the perinatal period	23 493
5	Influenza and pneumonia (J10 - J18)	19 135	5	Cerebrovascular diseases	19 948
6	Chronic lower respiratory diseases (J40 - J47)	12 573	6	Influenza and pneumonia	19 135
7	Diabetes mellitus (E10 - E14)	12 540	7	Chronic lower respiratory diseases	12 573
8	Ischaemic heart diseases (I20 - I25)	11 426	8	Diabetes mellitus	12 540
9	Intestinal infectious diseases (A00 - A09)	11 155	9	Accidents (unintentional injuries)	11 014
10	*Human immunodeficiency virus [HIV] diseases (B20 - B24)*	*9 925*	10	*Human immunodeficiency virus (HIV) disease*	*9 925*
	Other causes	193 734		Nonrankable causes	107 296
				Other rankable causes	62 040
	All causes	381 902		All causes	381 902

Source: Appendix D, *Mortality and causes of death in South Africa, 1997-2003: Findings from death notifications.* In: Africa SS, ed. Pretoria, South Africa: Statistics South Africa, Pretoria; 2005

11.2. Appendix B: Underlying vs. Causes of Death: *1997, 1999,* and *2001*

Table 17 – Underlying Cause vs. reported Causes of Death: 1997, 1999, and 2001

Rank	Underlying and reported causes of death	Rank No. of deaths due to this underlying cause	No. of forms with this recorded cause	%
	1997			
1	Tuberculosis (A15 - A19)	22 021	25 640	85.89
2	Other forms of heart disease (I30 – I52)	20 103	60 768	33.08
3	Cerebrovascular diseases (I60 - I69)	16 992	24 039	70.69
4	Influenza and pneumonia (J10 - J18)	11 503	24 698	46.57
5	Diabetes mellitus (E10 - E14)	10 828	12 133	89.24
6	Chronic lower respiratory diseases (J40 - J47)	10 747	15 330	70.10
7	Ischaemic heart diseases (I20 - I25)	9 794	14 512	67.49
8	Malignant neoplasms of digestive organs (C15 - C26)	8 914	9 499	93.84
9	Hypertensive diseases (I10 - I15)	7 706	19 786	38.95
10	Respiratory and cardiovascular disorders specific to the perinatal period (P20 - P29)	7 125	15 449	46.12
	1999			
1	Tuberculosis (A15 - A19)	34 173	39 759	85.95
2	Other forms of heart disease (I30 – I52)	20 120	53 977	37.28
3	Cerebrovascular diseases (I60 - I69)	19 948	28 218	70.69
4	Influenza and pneumonia (J10 - J18)	19 135	39 069	48.98
5	Chronic lower respiratory diseases (J40 - J47)	12 573	18 242	68.92
6	Diabetes mellitus (E10 - E14)	12 540	14 244	88.04
7	Ischaemic heart diseases (I20 - I25)	11 426	16 867	67.74
8	Intestinal infectious diseases (A00 - A09)	11 155	13 206	84.47
9	Human immunodeficiency virus [HIV] diseases (B20 – B24)	9 925	10 331	96.07
10	Hypertensive diseases (I10 - I15)	9 427	24 911	37.84
	2001			
1	Tuberculosis (A15 - A19)	50 872	56 985	89.27
2	Influenza and pneumonia (J10 - J18)	31 495	55 115	57.14
3	Other forms of heart diseases (I30 - I52)	22 602	48 927	46.20
4	Cerebrovascular diseases (I60 - I69)	22 577	31 104	72.59
5	Intestinal infectious diseases (A00 - A09)	16 060	18 241	88.04
6	Chronic lower respiratory diseases (J40 - J47)	14 681	20 136	72.91
7	Diabetes mellitus (E10 - E14)	14 557	16 207	89.82
8	Ischaemic heart diseases (I20 - I25)	11 777	17 380	67.76
9	Certain disorders involving the immune mechanism (D80 - D89)	11 670	20 345	57.36
10	Hypertensive diseases (I10 - I15)	10 748	27 622	38.91

Source: Table 4.16, *Mortality and causes of death in South Africa, 1997-2003: Findings from death notifications.* In: Africa SS, ed. Pretoria, South Africa: Statistics South Africa, Pretoria; 2005

11.3. Appendix C: The RSA Death Notification Data Set, 1997–2008

Table 17 lists the annual number of deaths in the RSA from 1997–2008. The annual number of deaths increased over time. RSA attributed this increase to a 10% growth in population over this period and improvements in death registration.

In 1997, the review process for deriving the underlying cause of death from death notifications became entirely automatic. Deaths notifications that cannot be processed automatically were processed by hand.

Estimations for the completeness of the death registration process are from 1997 to 2008. For the years 1997–2003, Statistics South Africa estimated 90% coverage. The estimated percentage decreased over time to reach 81% by the 2008 annual report.

Table 18 – Annual Number of RSA Death Notifications, 1997–2008

Year of Death	Total Number of Deaths*	Automatic Derivation Underlying Cause of Death	Estimated Completeness (Representation of all Actual Deaths)	Cause of Death "unclassified"**
1997	317 132	98%	90%	13.5%
1998	365 853	98%	90%	—
1999	381 820	98%	90%	12.4%
2000	416 155	98%	90%	—
2001	454 882	98%	90%	—
2002	502 050	98%	90% males • 87% females	—
2003	556 779	—	87% males • 82% females	12%
2004	576 709	—	90% males • 88% females	12%
2005	598 131	99.2%	85% males • 79% females	12,2%
2006	612 778	99.6%	86% males • 79% females	13.5%
2007	603 094	98.3%	85% males • 77% females	13.9%
2008	592 073	99.3%	81% for all deaths	13,6%

* by September 2010
** symptoms, signs and abnormal clinical and laboratory findings, not elsewhere classified (ICD-10 code: R00–R99)

Source: *Mortality and causes of death in South Africa, Findings from death notification* reports for 1997-2003, 2005, 2006, 2007, and 2008; Statistics South Africa, Pretoria.

Generally, over 50% of death notifications listed only one cause of death. By way of example, in 2008, the majority of death notification forms (59,6%) had only one cause recorded, just over a quarter (26,8%) had two causes recorded, 10,0% had three causes recorded and 3,5%

had four to five causes recorded. The pattern of recording causes on the death notification forms for 2008 is similar to that observed for 2007 deaths.[9]

The death notification form makes provision for a certifying official to indicate the method that was used to ascertain the cause of death. Table 18 shows that in about half of the deaths the causes of death were ascertained by opinions of medical personnel (33,7% opinion of the attending medical practitioner, 17,2% opinion of attending medical practitioner on duty and 2,0% opinion of registered professional nurse). An interview with family members was used to certify the cause of death for 15.5% of the deaths while an autopsy was used in less than 10% (8.6%) of the deaths. Where the occurrence of death could not be certified by a medical practitioner, an alternate form is completed by an induna (chief/headman) to certify the death and to provide a description of circumstances that led to and caused the death. It was unknown, or not indicated, in about one in five deaths (20,7%) what method was used to ascertain the cause of death.[9]

Table 19 - Method of Ascertaining Cause of Death, 2008

Method of Ascertaining Cause of Death	Number	Percentage
Autopsy	50,808	8.6 %
Opinion of attending medical practitioner	199,720	33.7 %
Opinion of attending medical practitioner on duty	101,645	17.2 %
Opinion of registered professional nurse	12,037	2.0 %
Interview of family member	91,655	15.5 %
Other	13,743	2.3 %
Unspecified	122,465	20.7 %
Total	592,073	100.0 %

Source: The *"Mortality and causes of death in South Africa, Findings from death notification"* reports for 1997-2003, 2005, 2006, 2007, and 2008; Statistics South Africa, Pretoria.

A substantial portion of all deaths cannot exactly be classified to a specific disease. They are relegated to the code: *symptoms, signs and abnormal clinical findings not elsewhere classified* (R00-R99). Over the years, roughly 13% of all deaths notifications are attributed to this code. For example, for the year 2008, a total of 80,515 deaths (13.6% of all deaths) were classified under symptoms, signs and abnormal clinical and laboratory findings, not elsewhere classified. Over 90% (94.4%) of these were *ill-defined and unknown causes of mortality*, a group which includes sudden infant death syndrome, other sudden death with cause unknown, unattended death, and any other ill-defined and unspecified causes of mortality. Although in some years, the code *symptoms, signs and abnormal clinical findings not elsewhere classified* would have been among the ten leading underlying causes, it is excluded from the ranking.[9, 11]

Statistics South Africa also cited the probable under-registration of deaths, particularly in rural areas and of children, as another limitation of the data used in this study.[11]

11.4. Appendix D: HIV/AIDS in the RSA Health System

As of 2008, the Republic of South Africa has an extensive public medical system comprised of 369 district hospitals, 54 regional hospitals, 12 tertiary/academics hospitals, and 9 central hospitals that specialize in specific diseases, such as tuberculosis or psychiatric disorders. All together, the RSA public health system contains a total of 87,870 public hospital beds.

In addition, the RSA public health care system has 3077 clinics, most providing 24-hour service, that provide "one-stop" medical service and referrals to hospitals; plus 313 community health centers which are clinics on a bigger scale.

The clinics and community centers provide free health services. Hospitals are free for children under 6 years of age, pregnant women, people on pensions, and people with communicable diseases, such as HIV infection and tuberculosis. Free, voluntary, HIV antibody tests are available at the 3077 public health clinics and 313 community health centers. HIV testing is accompanied by pre-test and post-test counseling. HIV infection is not a notifiable disease in the RSA.[15] Medical treatment of communicable diseases is free in the RSA public health care system; therefore, treatment of HIV/AIDS is free. Free medical treatment is available for children under 6 years of age, pregnant women, and pensioners.

The Republic of South Africa also has 212 private hospitals containing a total of nearly 9000 beds.[*]

---

[*] Personal communication with Statistics South Africa

11.5. Appendix E: The 1982 CDC Case Definition for AIDS

Excerpted from: *Update on acquired immune deficiency syndrome (AIDS)--United States.* Morbidity and Mortality Weekly Report. Sep 24, 1982; 31(37): 507-508, 513-514.[22]

CDC defines a case of AIDS as a disease, at least moderately predictive of a defect in cell-mediated immunity, occurring in a person with no known cause for diminished resistance to that disease. Such diseases include KS, PCP, and serious OIs [opportunistic infections]. Diagnoses are considered to fit the case definition only if based on sufficiently reliable methods (generally histology or culture). However, this case definition may not include the full spectrum of AIDS manifestations, which may range from absence of symptoms (despite laboratory evidence of immune deficiency) to non-specific symptoms (e.g., fever, weight loss, generalized, persistent lymphadenopathy) (4) to specific diseases that are insufficiently predictive of cellular immunodeficiency to be included in incidence monitoring (e.g., tuberculosis, oral candidiasis, herpes zoster) to malignant neoplasms that cause, as well as result from, immunodeficiency((P)) (5). Conversely, some patients who are considered AIDS cases on the basis of diseases only moderately predictive of cellular immunodeficiency may not actually be immunodeficient and may not be part of the current epidemic. Absence of a reliable, inexpensive, widely available test for AIDS, however, may make the working case definition the best currently available for incidence monitoring.

Two points in this update deserve emphasis. First, the eventual case-mortality rate of AIDS, a few years after diagnosis, may be far greater than the 41% overall case-mortality rate noted above. Second, the reported incidence of AIDS has continued to increase rapidly. Only a small percentage of cases have none of the identified risk factors (male homosexuality, intravenous drug abuse, Haitian origin, and perhaps hemophilia A). To avoid a reporting bias, physicians should report cases regardless of the absence of these factors.

Physicians aware of patients fitting the case definition for AIDS are requested to report such cases to CDC through their local or state health departments

— HIV was added to the Centers for Disease Control Case Definition in 1985 [156] —

11.6. Appendix F: The South African HIV Club – Blacks Only

Health outcomes in the Republic of South Africa (RSA) are stratified by population group. The racial breakdowns are African, White, Indian/Asian, and Colored. Per RSA death notifications, HIV infection is an exclusively African Black phenomenon.

Tables 19 and 20 lists the ten leading natural underlying causes of death by population group in 1999 and 2008, respectively. In 1999, black Africans were the only population group to have HIV/AIDS deaths.[11] In 2008, black Africans were the only population group to have HIV/AIDS deaths, excepting 8 HIV/AIDS deaths in the unknown population group category. Between 2003 and 2008, inclusive, the only HIV/AIDS deaths tabulated in the RSA were among African blacks: no HIV/AIDS deaths were reported among White, Indian/Asian or Colored populations for these years.[2, 7, 9, 11-13] (This parameter was not published consistently every year.)

From Statistics South Africa's point of view: "We code what we see." Statistics South Africa assumes the absence of HIV among the White population is due to their access to private hospitals and physicians. HIV/AIDS is not a notifiable disease in the RSA – physicians are not required to report it.[15] Statistics South Africa assumes that "people don't want to disadvantage their family" and/or "lose their life insurance," so cooperative private physicians evidently write down "the immediate cause" of death (i.e., the opportunistic infection), and not "AIDS" on the death notification form. A greater percentage of [African blacks] "don't mind" that their HIV or AIDS status is recorded because "they have nothing to lose." People with communicable diseases receive free health care in the public RSA health care system.[*]

---

[*] Personal communication with Statistics South Africa

Table 20 – Ten Leading Underlying Causes of Death by Population Group, 1999

Causes of death (based on the Tenth Revision, International Classification of Diseases, 1992)	Black African			Colored			Indian/Asian			White			Unknown/Unspecified		
	Rank	Number	%	Rank	Number	%	Rank	Number	%	Rank	Number	%	Rank	Number	%
All causes		215 699	100.0		22 987	100.0		4 773	100.0		32 823	100.0	...	105 620	100.0
Tuberculosis (A15 - A19)	1	22 780	10.6	1	1 717	7.5	8	95	2.0	...	...	...	1	9 401	8.9
Influenza and pneumonia (J10 - J18)	2	12 562	5.8	10	532	2.3	9	93	1.9	7	1 165	3.5	4	4 783	4.5
Cerebrovascular diseases (I60 - I69)	3	10 960	5.1	2	1 565	6.8	4	263	5.5	3	2 126	6.5	3	5 034	4.8
Other forms of heart disease (I30 - I52)	4	10 886	5.0	6	1 094	4.8	3	266	5.6	2	2 131	6.5	2	5 743	5.4
Intestinal infectious diseases (A00 - A09)	5	7 517	3.5	...	...	...	...	...	...	...	...	...	6	3 202	3.0
HIV diseases (B20 - B24)	*6*	*7 033*	*3.3*	...	...	...	...	...	...	...	...	...	...	...	...
Chronic lower respiratory diseases (J40 - J47)	7	6 246	2.9	5	1 108	4.8	5	191	4.0	4	1 832	5.6	7	3 196	3.0
Certain disorders of immune mechanism (D80 - D89)	8	6 206	2.9	...	...	...	...	...	...	...	...	...	...	...	...
Hypertensive diseases (I10 - I15)	9	5 827	2.7	9	541	2.4	6	140	2.9	9	682	2.1	...	...	...
Diabetes mellitus (E10 – E14)	10	5 754	2.7	3	1 233	5.4	1	757	15.9	6	1 385	4.2	5	3 411	3.2
Malignant neoplasms of digestive organs (C15 - C26)	...	...	...	8	813	5.1	7	131	2.7	5	1 641	5.0	9	2 467	2.3
Ischaemic heart diseases (I20 - I25)	...	...	...	4	1 176	5.1	2	578	12.1	1	4 471	13.6	8	2 556	2.4
Malign. neoplasms of resp. & intrathor. organs (C30 - C39)	...	...	...	7	871	3.9	9	93	1.9	8	1 071	3.3	...	...	...
Renal failure (N17 - N19)	...	...	...	...	...	...	10	91	1.9	...	...	...	...	...	...
Malign. neoplasms of ill-defined, sec. & unspecified site (C76 - C80)	...	...	...	...	...	...	...	...	...	10	643	2.0	...	...	...
Resp. & cardiovascular disorders - perinatal (P20 - P29)	...	...	...	...	...	...	...	...	...	...	...	...	10	2 337	2.2
Other causes		119 928	55.6		12 337	53.7		2 075	43.5		15 676	47.8		63 490	24.0

Source: Appendix H, *Mortality and causes of death in South Africa, 1997–2003: Findings from death notifications.* In: Africa SS, ed. Pretoria, South Africa: Statistics South Africa, Pretoria; 2005.

Table 21 – Ten Leading Underlying Causes of Death by Population Group, 2008

Causes of death (based on the Tenth Revision, International Classification of Diseases, 1992)	Black African			White			Indian/Asian			Colored			Unknown/Unspecified		
	Rank	Number	%	Rank	Number	%	Rank	Number	%	Rank	Number	%	Rank	Number	%
Tuberculosis (A15-A19)*	1	54 186	14,7	...	...	...	9	199	2,7	1	2 424	9,6	1	17 767	11,4
Influenza and pneumonia (J10-J18)	2	33 648	9,1	6	1 602	4,5	10	189	2,5	10	807	3,2	2	9 356	6,0
Intestinal infectious diseases (A00-A09)	3	29 780	8,1	...	...	...	...	...	...	...	...	...	3	8 720	5,6
Other forms of heart disease (I30-I52)	4	16 305	4,4	2	2 441	6,8	3	558	7,5	6	1 015	4,0	4	5 871	3,8
Cerebrovascular diseases (I60-I69)	5	15 271	4,1	3	2 024	5,6	4	373	5,0	5	1 340	5,3	5	5 355	3,4
Human immunodeficiency virus [HIV] disease (B20-B24)	6	11 069	3,0	...	...	...	...	...	...	...	...	...	8	3 316	2,1
Certain disorders involving the immune mechanism (D80-D89)	7	11 038	3,0	...	...	...	...	...	...	...	...	...	9	3 218	2,1
Diabetes mellitus (E10-E14)	8	10 815	2,9	7	1 552	4,3	1	1 049	14,1	2	1 595	6,3	6	4 547	2,9
Hypertensive diseases (I10-I15)	9	9 311	2,5	9	852	2,4	7	217	2,9	8	891	3,5	...	...	...
Other viral diseases (B25-B34)	10	8 098	2,2	...	...	...	...	...	...	...	...	...	10	3 172	2,0
Ischaemic heart diseases (I20-I25)	...	...	...	1	4 418	12,3	2	983	13,2	4	1 416	5,6	...	...	...
Malignant neoplasm of digestive organs (C15-C26)	...	...	...	4	1 922	5,4	6	228	3,1	9	853	3,4	...	...	...
Chronic lower respiratory diseases (J40-J47)	...	...	...	5	1 793	5,0	5	257	3,5	3	1 424	5,6	7	3 382	2,2
Malignant neoplasm of respiratory and intrathoracic organs (C30-39)	...	...	...	8	1 266	3,5	...	...	...	7	914	3,6	...	...	...
Renal failure (N17-N19)	...	...	...	10	804	2,2	8	207	2,8	...	...	...	...	...	...
Other natural causes		134 928	36,7		13 902	38,8		2 427	32,7		9 669	38,3		78 359	50,4
Non-natural		33 634	9,1		3 284	9,2		740	10,0		2 913	11,5		12 379	8,0
All causes		368 083	100,0		35 860	100,0		7 427	100,0		25 261	100,0		155 442	100,0

*Including deaths due to multidrug-resistant tuberculosis (MDR TB) and extremely drug-resistant tuberculosis (XDR-TB)

Source: Appendix M.1, *Mortality and causes of death in South Africa, 2008: Findings from death notification.* In: Africa SS, ed. Pretoria, South Africa: Statistics South Africa, Pretoria; 2010.

Notes

Notes

Notes